AGAINST THE TIDE

Career Paths of Women Leaders in American and British Higher Education

edited by
Karen Doyle Walton

Published by
Phi Delta Kappa Educational Foundation

Cover design by
Victoria Voelker

Cover illustration by
Karen Stolper

Phi Delta Kappa Educational Foundation
408 North Union Street
Post Office Box 789
Bloomington, Indiana 47402-0789
U.S.A.

Printed in the United States of America

Library of Congress Catalog Card Number 96-68619
ISBN 0-87367-490-1

Acknowledgments

This book was made possible by four mentors. Reverend Daniel G. Gambet, OSFS, president of Allentown College of St. Francis de Sales, and Reverend Alexander T. Pocetto, OSFS, senior vice president, have given me guidance, encouragement, and marvelous opportunities to learn the craft of higher education administration. Most notable are my experiences at the Harvard Institute for Educational Management; a term as Visiting Scholar at Wolfson College, Cambridge University; and a Fulbright Administrative Fellowship at La Sainte Union College of Higher Education in Southampton, England. The other mentors are, of course, my parents, Dr. and Mrs. Albert F. Doyle. These four persons have been profound role models — healers of spirit and body, pursuers of the intellect and the human, and purveyors of kindness beyond measure. To thank them will require a lifetime.

Table of Contents

Introduction

Against the Tide records the distinctive voices of 20 women who describe their personal journeys to top positions of leadership in higher education. Ten American and 10 British heads of colleges and universities tell their unique stories about cracking the "glass ceiling" that many observers believe exists and often limits career leadership opportunities for women in academe.

For convenience, in this introduction I refer to these women as "presidents," though their actual titles include principal, mistress, vice-chancellor, and other terms. *President* conveys the right notion of leadership and responsibility for their institutions.

In the fall of 1992, I was a visiting scholar at Wolfson College, Cambridge University, and a United Kingdom Fulbright Administrative Fellow at La Sainte Union College of Higher Education in Southampton, England. During a three-month period, I interviewed women chief executive officers of English institutions of higher education, including all the women heads of the colleges of Cambridge and Oxford Universities. Although each visit was preceded by only a letter of introduction from the United Kingdom Fulbright Commission, my *curriculum vitae,* and a brief cover letter explaining the purpose of the interview, in each case I was welcomed with warm hospitality. Contrary to American popular opinion concerning British restraint and formality, the interviewees were candid and engaging. At the conclusion of the interview, I invited each president to contribute a chapter to a collection of profiles. Encouraged by the cordial British reception, I later used a similar procedure with women presidents of American colleges and universities. The result is this book.

These insightful, often revealing essays are intended not only to provide an ethnographic snapshot of women who have reached the highest rung on the ladder of higher education administration but also to give the reader an opportunity to search for patterns and models among the various career paths of these individuals. One might ask, for example, whether the essays of the British presidents reveal common leadership characteristics and experiences among that group that differ from the characteristics and experiences of their American counterparts. Is the leadership ability of these women innate or acquired; and, in either case, what development or mentoring activities nurtured their leadership talents?

In addition to examining the commonalities and contrasts among the various career paths of these women, the reader also may discern emerging management styles. *Against the Tide* is not intended merely for a narrow audience of aspiring American and British women in higher education administration. Nor is it intended solely for more general readers in higher education, though such readers will likely find these profiles instructive. Rather, students, researchers, and scholars of leadership development theory across national, vocational, and avocational boundaries can extract lessons about the conduits to leadership for both men and women in academe. Likewise, casual readers, as well as scholars in the field of women's studies, will find ideas worthy of contemplation and further examination.

These women presidents have, in many cases, traveled uncommon paths. They have swum against the prevailing tides of historical practice and the status quo. Many readers will see these women's challenges as daunting. But, by recording their singular struggles and achievements, the writers of *Against the Tide* have set down strategies and philosophies for other women (and men) to consider and, perhaps, to follow.

Background Information

In 1985 the American Council on Education's (ACE) Office of Women in Higher Education (OWHE) conducted the first comprehensive survey of women college and university presidents in the United States. The study addressed personal and demographic information, career paths, the search process, job satisfaction, and attitudes about women's and minority issues of all female chief executive officers at institutions of higher education. The researchers, Judith Touchton, Donna Shavlik (deputy director and

2

director, respectively, of the OWHE), and Lynne Davis, provided baseline data from which women presidents could be studied by institutional sector (for example, public versus independent institutions, two-year versus four-year, and so on). That survey, which was sent to all women presidents of two- and four-year colleges and universities accredited by one of the six regional accrediting bodies, produced an 88% response; and the findings were published in *Women in Presidencies: A Descriptive Study of Women College and University Presidents* in 1993.

In July 1995, Dr. Touchton and Deborah Ingram, Coordinator of Women's Programs at the OWHE, updated the 1985 study and reported some 20-year trends. The 1995 data highlight the following substantial gains for women presidents over that period:

- A total of 453 women, representing 16% of all presidents, head regionally accredited colleges and universities in the United States, compared with 148 (6%) two decades earlier.
- Slightly less than half (48%) of all women presidents are in public colleges and universities, which represents a dramatic change from 11% in 1975 and 36% in 1984.
- Of all women presidents, 3 out of 5 are in 4-year colleges and universities, and 2 out of 5 are in 2-year institutions.
- Women presidents in 1995 were racially and ethnically diverse. Of the 453 women CEOs, 16% were women of color: 39 African-American, 24 Hispanic, 7 Native American, and 2 Asian-American. These data represent a significant increase since 1985, when only 7% of female presidents were women of color.
- Women presidents serve in all sizes of colleges and universities: 71% head institutions with enrollments less than 3,000; 22% in institutions with enrollments between 3,000 and 10,000; and 7% in institutions with enrollments in excess of 10,000.

The following table from *Women Presidents in U.S. Colleges and Universities: A 1995 Higher Education Update* (published by the American Council on Education Office of Women in

3

Higher Education) documents the steady increase in the percentage of women chief executive officers over the last 20 years.

Number of Women Chief Executive Officers at Institutions, Branch and Affiliated Campuses Selected Years, 1975-1995*

Institutional Type (as of)	1975 (12/31/75)	1984 (12/31/84)	1992 (4/15/92)	1995 (4/15/95)
Private	132	182	184	237
4-Year	98	134	154	199
2-Year	34	48	30	38
Public	16	104	164	216
4-Year	5	32	58	78
2-Year	11	72	106	138
Total Women CEOs	148	286	348	453
Total Number of Institutions	2500	2800	3000	2903
Percentage of Women CEOs	6%	10%	12%	16%

*From Judith Touchton and Deborah Ingram, *Women Presidents in U.S. Colleges and Universities: A 1995 Higher Education Update* (Washington, D.C.: American Council on Education, 1995). Used with permission.

With respect to personal background, the 1985 ACE survey (Touchton, Shavlik, and Davis 1993) found that the ages of the women presidents ranged from 36 to 73, with median age of 51. Their religions were 50% Catholic, 37% Protestant, and 4% Jewish. The marital status of the respondents was 50% single (never married), 32% married, 14% separated or divorced, 4% widowed, and 1% had a committed partner. Of the lay presidents, 54% reported having children.

Graduates of women's colleges represented 40% of the respondents to the 1985 survey, and 63% of the women presidents of four-year independent institutions were alumnae of women's colleges. The highest degree earned by 1% of the respondents was a bachelor's degree, 17% a master's degree, 62% a Ph.D., 16% an

4

Ed.D., 3% other professional degrees, and 1% gave no response. Twenty-eight percent of the respondents had served in higher education for 16 to 20 years. Almost three-quarters had risen to the position of president from other presidencies, vice presidencies, or other positions in academic affairs.

Other professional backgrounds included participation in leadership development activities, such as the ACE National Identification Program (37%), ACE's National Forum (28%), Harvard University's Institute for Educational Management (15%), AAWCJC leadership development programs (11%), and the ACE Fellows Program (9%).

The majority of the women president respondents (57%) were highly satisfied with their jobs; 39% were satisfied; and 3% were only somewhat satisfied. When asked about their career plans for the next three to five years, the majority said they would most likely remain in their current jobs, with the most viable other option being another presidency (39%).

When the three ACE researchers compared male and female presidents in 1985, they found the two groups to be of approximately the same age, with similar educational backgrounds and career paths. However, a far higher percentage of lay male presidents (93%) than lay female presidents (48%) were married, and women presidents had far higher divorce and separation rates.

Although only about 25% of married women in the United States worked outside the home in 1950, 44% of the women presidents' mothers were in the labor force before their daughters had graduated from high school during that era. The authors remarked that the mothers of the women presidents "seem to have served as early role models for career pursuit and achievement" (Touchton, Shavlik, and Davis 1993). The OWHE *1995 Higher Education Update* does not include corresponding data concerning the women presidents' educational and personal backgrounds, career paths, and job satisfaction.

No similar studies of women presidents of British universities and colleges exist, perhaps because there is no English counterpart of the ACE Office of Women in Higher Education, but more likely because few women have held the top posts of president, vice-chancellor, principal, or mistress in Great Britain. However, my research on the eight women who were serving as heads of Oxbridge (Oxford and Cambridge) colleges during 1992-93 and the only two women who were serving as vice-chancellors in the British university system during that academic year, does provide some basis of comparison of American and British female presidents. The five Cambridge colleges headed by females in 1992, listed in order of the establishment of the college, were Girton (1869), Newnham (1871), Homerton (1894), New Hall (1954), and Lucy Cavendish (1965). Although all five were founded as women's colleges, only Newnham, New Hall, and Lucy Cavendish remain so. Oxford colleges with female principals in 1992 were Somerville (1879), St. Anne's (1893), and St. Hilda's (1893), with only St. Hilda's remaining a women's college by 1995. The two other universities (formerly polytechnics) included in the 1992 study were South Bank and Sunderland.

The five Cambridge colleges with women heads ranged in total enrollment from 91 to 633, with an average enrollment of 414 and a median enrollment of 462. The average 1990-91 enrollment of the three Oxford colleges with women principals was 366, and the median enrollment was 350. As a basis of comparison, the average total enrollment of all 31 Cambridge colleges in 1990-91 was 486, and the average enrollment of the total 38 Oxford colleges was 332 (Bell 1991; Bryson 1995; Ormrod 1992). South Bank University had approximately 20,000 students and Sunderland University had approximately 7,000 at this time. Admittedly, the 31 colleges that compose Cambridge University and the 38 Oxford colleges are institutionally quite different from colleges and universities in the United States. As one female principal explained:

> Oxbridge colleges are elements of a large University, with major research ambitions in every field. The Colleges provide an institutional structure that is orthogonal to University structures, and which deliver a range of academic and ancillary services, but by no means a full range. In particu-

lar, the students at these colleges obtain their degrees from the University, are examined by the University, and must meet University standards in all respects.

The American institutions, on the other hand, are self-contained, providing a complete range of services and granting their own degrees. The 1994 enrollments of the 10 American colleges and universities represented in this volume range from a low of 1,059 students to a high of 22,700, with a mean of 8,049 and a median of 2,826 students.

Biographical information about 10 of the 11 British principals included in the 1992 study (six of whom contributed chapters to this book) was found in *Who's Who 1992,* which revealed that their average age was 57, their median age was 59 (excluding the one retired principal), and all were Caucasian. The average number of years the British principals had held their present office was 4, and the median was 3 (again excluding the retiree). Although they were not asked their marital status, 7 of the 11 mentioned they were married (1 of whom also stated she was divorced), 4 referred to their children (numbering from 1 to 4), and one alluded to 4 grandchildren.

Admittedly, Oxford and Cambridge are unlike the rest of British higher education. Gillian T. Cell, provost of the College of William and Mary and an English historian who came to the United States in the 1960s, has noted: "The pattern of appointing heads of colleges from the civil service, the diplomatic service, politics, etc., is not typical outside Oxbridge; elsewhere vice-chancellors are almost invariably academics."

An Overview of the Issues

Each of the 20 women presidents included in this book was asked to write an autobiographical essay addressing some or all of the following matters: personal background, educational background, career path, helps (such as mentors) and hindrances encountered, recruitment for her present position, scholarly activities, public activities, acquiring and developing her leadership style and skills, personal strengths, conflict management, stress, job satisfaction, and encouraging other women to pursue careers in higher education administration. Each author was given wide latitude in terms of the content and format of her essay so as to encourage the writing of an essay distinctly reflecting the writer's personality and style. In short, each woman was encouraged to tell her story "in her own voice."

Educational and Family Backgrounds. The educational backgrounds of the American writers in this volume differ, as a group, from those of the British writers. All of the Americans hold earned doctorates, and only two attended women's colleges as undergraduates. Their academic fields include anthropology, chemistry, English, geography, history, linguistics, philosophy, special education, and zoology/parasitology.

In contrast, seven of the British presidents received bachelors' degrees from Oxford and Cambridge colleges that were single-sex institutions at the time of their attendance. Unique to Oxbridge is the practice of automatically conferring a master's degree three to six years after an individual has earned a bachelor's degree. This tradition of awarding a second degree without additional study or research is based on the assumption that the intervening years of life experience qualify the bachelor's recipient for a master's degree. The British writers who hold earned doctorates have academic specialties in chemistry (2 presidents), English literature, economics, and mathematics. Unlike their American counterparts, each of the British presidents attended a girls' school before entering college or university, which was considered typical in their youth.

Several American presidents worked their way through college (one, for example, as a babysitter, waitress, housecleaner, women's clothing store clerk, secretarial replacement in a tannery, and statistician in a meat packing plant). In contrast, only one British president mentioned working, as a nursing orderly in a hospital, prior to college.

8

More British than American writers' parents attended college. The grandfather of one British president was Warden of New College, Oxford, in the early 1900s and Vice Chairman of Lady Margaret Hall, Oxford, in 1910. An American author relates that her mother was President of the Wellesley College Alumnae Association. Several presidents from both sides of the Atlantic mention that their fathers left secondary school early to become a clerk, garage mechanic, or other blue-collar worker. However, no strong correlation emerges between the extent of their parents' formal education and their encouragement of their daughters to pursue higher education. One American president whose mother was rarely home credits her father as being "the parent of influence essentially for the first 10 years of my life." Despite a physical injury and limited education, "he loved learning and wanted his children to love books and intellectual challenge."

One American president considered her mother, who taught at the girls' school she attended, one of two female role models who gave her "the gifts of their experience, example, and encouragement . . . not by relating to me their life stories but by allowing me to live and work for some years in their presence." The mother of an Oxford principal pointed out constantly that she had "given up everything" for her daughter and, therefore, the child had to achieve something to compensate for this. That principal recollects no mentors or role models, and it is unfortunate that neither parent lived to see her reach her present stature on the highest rung of British higher education. Two presidents, coincidentally, hold doctorates in chemistry from Oxford. One of these presidents cites as a role model Dorothy Crowfoot Hodgkin, who won a Nobel Prize in chemistry and reared "rough-and-tumble children. . . . Yet neither of her two roles appeared to negate the other!"

Approximately half of the women in this volume are married and have children (ranging in number from 1 to 4); one has 4 grandchildren, and more than one has been divorced.

Career Paths and Recruitment. The career paths of the American women are, in general, steps up the academic ladder: faculty member, department chair, academic dean or vice president, and then president. Although several of their British counterparts rose from academic backgrounds, others gained prominence in Her Majesty's Diplomatic Service, with one recruited from her post as Ambassador to Luxembourg to become mistress of a Cambridge college. Another British writer was invited to apply for the position of principal by the Fellows of an Oxford college during her successful career as a civil servant.

In a 6 November 1992 issue of the *Times Higher Education Supplement*, Baroness Pauline Perry refers to professorships as the "natural breeding ground for the post of vice-chancellor." She laments that because less than 4% of British professors are women, senior positions in colleges and universities attract very few female applicants. Perry characterizes the world of higher education as a "male club" and asserts, "For a woman to pull out of the crowd and to move up the ladder of management responsibility is extremely difficult."

A survey conducted by the Association of University Teachers (AUT) found that, in addition to the low percentage of female professors in the United Kingdom, female professors earn £2,000 per annum less than their male counterparts. This salary discrepancy previously had been attributed to the fact that more women teach in the "soft disciplines" that pay lower salaries, but the AUT survey found that female professors fared badly in *all* areas. Alison Utley (1991) argued that "more than half of all women professors (53%) earned less than £30,000 while the figure for men was 28%." Hence from a financial standpoint, British professorships are not particularly alluring, "natural breeding grounds" for nurturing women who aspire to the position of principal of colleges and universities.

The common procedure for recruiting a British college principal is for the governing fellows of the college to develop a pool of candidates through such means as searching in *Who's Who,* using headhunters, networking, nominations from friends and colleagues of candidates, and seeking self-nominations. Some British women principals replied to a public advertisement of the post. Several women believed that their heightened visibility through university committee work, foreign service, and other government posts enhanced their likelihood of being nominated or being asked to apply for the position of principal. The American presidents were recruited or applied for their positions following similar procedures.

Higher Education Administration as a Profession. In 1991 and 1993 the Pew Charitable Trusts sponsored three international roundtable discussions at which 24 "university citizens" from 12 countries on both sides of the Atlantic assessed the challenges and opportunities now facing universities. Two members of the transatlantic dialogue were Robert Atwell and Madeleine Green, president and vice president respectively of the American Council on Education. Green and Atwell believe that U.S. education institutions are less resistant to reform because of a "managerial class of presidents, vice-presidents, and deans, who see themselves not as professors briefly dabbling in administration but as executives engaged in academic enterprises . . ." They argue that the continental European process of electing rectors by professors and students and of empowering faculty senates makes reform difficult. The presidents of American institutions have little direct power, but they have more leverage than their European counterparts through budgetary authority, executive powers delegated to them by their boards of trustees, and connections with external constituencies (Green and Atwell 1993).

Dame Rosemary Murray, retired vice-chancellor of Cambridge University and principal of a Cambridge college, does not consider being principal of a college to be an eminent profession for a British man or woman. She feels that academic administration is not a career, and that academicians regard a professorship as the ultimate goal. Head of college is a post one assumes after having held other career posts.

This practice is illustrated by Dame Anne Warburton, who announced her retirement as president of Lucy Cavendish College of Cambridge University effective at the end of the 1993-94 academic year, marking the end of her third successful career, one

11

having been Ambassador to Denmark. Dame Rosemary Murray's opinion is echoed by a current Oxford principal who stated that "any Oxford academic who spends a great deal of time on administration, as I do, always faces jibes that those who choose to do this are failed academics." No similar disdain for academic administration was expressed by the American presidents, several of whom have attended professional development programs for higher education administrators, such as the prestigious Harvard Institute for Educational Management.

Terms and Conditions of Employment. The terms of employment vary greatly from Oxbridge to America. Mrs. Ruth Deech of St. Anne's College explains the federal nature of Oxford University by comparing its structure with that of the United States: "I am, as it were, governor of one of the states; but my post is mine until I reach the retirement age of 67, and there is virtually no way in which I can be dislodged." Ms. Elizabeth Llewellyn-Smith of St. Hilda's College relates that no job description or specific qualifications are presented for the head of an Oxford college. She comments that "the salary of a Principal, linked to the Oxford professional scale, would be regarded as risible in most professions and is a living wage only for someone with a pension from earlier employment or other means."

Salaries were not mentioned by the other British writers, and the only pertinent information that I found on this topic was in the *Cambridge Reporter* of 6 April 1992, which indicated that the salaries of female heads of Cambridge colleges were comparable to their male counterparts. Specifically, the 1990-91 salary of the head of Trinity College was £54,707, and the 1990-91 salary of the largest Cambridge college headed by a woman (total enrollment of 633) was £43,030. That source does not state what, if any, perquisites (such as housing, food, travel and entertainment budgets, and maid service) were provided to the heads of the various colleges in addition to their salaries.

The 1992-93 salaries of the six presidents of the American private colleges represented in this book average $124,800, from a low of $91,000 to a high of $149,290. When benefits are included, the total compensations of those six American presidents range from $101,280 to $179,449 with an average of $143,450. The 1992-93 salaries of the American presidents of public institutions were not readily available.

Fundraising and Job Satisfaction. The presidents of private colleges and universities in the United States candidly admit that the majority of their time is spent in activities directly or indirectly related to cultivating potential donors and acquiring gifts for their institution from private industrial firms. The British colleges and universities are funded by the federal government, but one Oxford president admits that she entertains guests at the college and spends a considerable part of her time on development activities — "very minor indeed on the American scale," according to her, "but, nonetheless, important and difficult." Another Oxford principal relates that "since all colleges are actively fundraising, increasing weight is placed today on the ability to motivate alumnae and top corporate or charitable sources of finance."

Job satisfaction is a shared trait of the writers, both British and American. One finds her post to be "immensely rewarding and enjoyable, with the opportunity to know and influence new generations of young people." A retired British principal found the position very stressful because of her responsibility "not only for the survival and success of the institution, but also for the individuals, both staff and students, who were involved." Nevertheless, she enjoyed her presidency and the "pleasure and exhilaration of working with a group of people who were not only generously supportive, but shared [her] ideals."

In describing her life, one British president advises readers to "try to keep yourself in perspective and not to take it all too seriously. Life is above all for living and not to enjoy it is a waste." Another, looking back over 43 years of a marriage, children, grandchildren, and professional life, concludes "*laeta sors mea* — happy is my lot."

Women Encouraging Women. Dame Rosemary Murray never has considered herself a feminist, but she always has encouraged other women to "do whatever they wanted." Dr. Katherine Pretty, principal of Homerton College, Cambridge University, who regards Dame Rosemary as her mentor, supports an extensive professional development program for her own faculty. Younger faculty who are experienced in current research and publication techniques give seminars to older faculty who wish to update their skills. She encourages women to serve on committees and pursue academic administration, acknowledging a women's network within the university that assists female colleagues in obtaining desired committee memberships.

Sian Griffiths (1991) described vice-chancellor Anne Wright's commitment to promoting equal opportunities at Sunderland University. After commissioning an audit of the percentages of women, ethnic minorities, and disabled students and staff, Dr. Wright took steps to improve Sunderland statistics, which she admits were in some cases worse than national averages. From 1989 to 1991, the percentage of women lecturers at Sunderland increased from 17.8% to 19.5%. (The national average was 22.9%.) During the same period, female principal lecturers rose from 7% to 10%, and female senior lecturers increased from 15% to 17%. Significant increases also were realized in the percentage of women in administrative staff positions. In particular, the percentage of female principal officers rose from 18.5% to 33.5% and senior officers from 57% to 69%. Dr. Wright has established training programs that include fair recruitment procedures, image and self-projection for women, and assertiveness (rather than aggressiveness) for men.

Baroness Pauline Perry traces her initiative and indefatigability back to her great-grandmother, the widow of a well-to-do ship's captain from Sunderland who was killed at sea. This industrious woman took in wash to support 11 children and to pay a penny a week for the principal's grandmother to attend the local dame school. The grandmother appreciated her mother's financial sacrifice and completed her studies one year early, at the age of 11, to lessen the monetary outlay. Baroness Perry's mother attended the London College of Music and determined that her daughter would matriculate in college. Baroness Perry also received encouragement from her father, the president of a theological college, who gave his seven-year-old daughter books by Jean-Jacques Rousseau and John Stuart Mills, which she gladly read (Ozga 1993).

Baroness Perry states that "perhaps the best aspect of the situation lies in one's ability to help other women up the steep-sided pyramid." She remains convinced that "networks are an essential support for women as they move into posts where responsibilities and painful isolation undermine their confidence." She warns against becoming exclusionary, advising instead that "both the world of work and the world of home are better when they are shared in equal partnership by men and women together, rather than when either tries to exclude the other." The response to "all-male clubs, the all-male organizations, the old-boys' networks" should not be to set up "all-female clubs and missions. Many women (though not all) have great talents in healing relationships and in creating new bridges: Their involvement in public life and in the marketplace should surely mean that sexism can be conquered and that the human race can acknowledge the spread of its many talents through male and female alike" (Ozga 1993).

An opposing view was expressed by a principal who feels that most women who have made it have had to be "honorary men." She observed that in order for a woman to reach the highest levels in civil service and concurrently to be a successful mother and wife, she would have to employ a "perfect nanny and housekeeper." In academic positions, the percentage of female professors is very low; and there is a preponderance of men in staff positions, except in areas consisting of "women's work." One principal remarked, "Some women think that if another woman has 'made it,' by definition she has betrayed her sisters." Another principal has always behaved

> as if equality between the sexes prevailed, to ignore barriers
> that may or may not exist, to forge ahead regardless, never

15

to espouse the "victim mentality," to believe that anything is possible, and to be robust in the face of alleged sexual and religious harassment. . . . It has worked very well for me and, equally, for others of my generation. Younger women seem to belong to a different species altogether, of a more sensitive and victimized nature; and as I get older, I find their attitude more and more inexplicable and self-defeating.

In addition to holding the top positions at their institutions, Baroness Tessa Blackstone and Baroness Perry are members of the House of Lords, which has only 5% female leadership.

Bridges Across the Atlantic

Polarity between the American and British presidents is diminished by the fact that several of them have built and crossed transatlantic bridges. The epitome is Dr. Paula Brownlee, whose American mother and English father sent her to Somerville College, Oxford, for her A.B. and M.A. degrees. After earning a D.Phil. in organic chemistry from Oxford, Dr. Brownlee completed a postdoctoral fellowship at the University of Rochester. She subsequently assumed the posts of tenured faculty member, dean of the faculty, and president of American colleges. Having received honorary degrees from 14 American colleges, British-born Dr. Brownlee draws on her bicultural background in her current position of president of the Association of American Colleges and Universities.

Other transatlantic experiences include Baroness Tessa Blackstone's visiting fellowship at Harvard University, Mrs. Ruth Deech's M.A. from Brandeis University, Professor Dorothy Wedderburn's visiting professorship at the Massachusetts Institute of Technology, and Dr. Carol Cartwright's research fellowship at Birkbeck College of the University of London. The oldest Anglo-American connection is Dr. Martha Church's ancestry, which goes back to John Alden, Priscilla Mullens, and Love Brewster, "all of Mayflower fame."

The first Women Presidents' Summit convened in 1990 with approximately 200 delegates, including two-thirds of the United

States' women presidents and 13 of the more than 100 women who hold similar positions abroad. The 1993 Women Presidents' Summit, held in Washington, D.C., had two major purposes: "to recognize the past achievements and future roles of women leaders, and to reframe major national and international issues in ways that place women at the center rather than on the periphery." That important meeting, sponsored by the American Council on Education in cooperation with 13 other presidential associations, brought together American and foreign women presidents to showcase their achievements and their growing influence in the United States and throughout the world. The daunting goal of that 1993 summit was "to develop a blueprint for action . . . to guide women presidents worldwide in their efforts to insure that women's voices will be heard on issues of importance to our respective nations and the world," such as war and peace, economics and the environment, and the intersection of public and private life (ACE 1993).

I find it heartening to envision women presidents from around the world joining forces to develop a new global agenda for peace and prosperity. The intelligence, integrity, and goodwill of the 20 American and British presidents represented in this volume give one hope that such a mission can be accomplished. As affirmed in the 1993 Women Presidents' Summit, such an image of connectedness "is conceptually, visually, intellectually, and bodily associated with life-giving force, a power philosophically and historically relegated to the private realm of women" (ACE 1993).

References

American Council on Education (ACE). "Overview of the 1993 Summit." Washington, D.C., 1993.

Bell, Brian. *Oxford Insight City Guides.* Singapore: APA Publications, 1991.

Bryson, Bill. "The Style and Substance of Oxford." *National Geographic* (April 1995).

Green, Madeleine F., and Atwell, Robert H. "A View from the United States: Forces for Change." *Policy Perspectives* 5, no. 1 (June 1993).

Griffiths, Sian. "Right Note with Women." *Times Higher Education Supplement*, 27 December 1991.

Ormrod, Sarah J. *The University of Cambridge: An Introduction.* Cambridge: University of Cambridge Board of Continuing Education, 1992.

Ozga, Jenny. *Women in Educational Management.* Buckingham: Open University Press, 1993.

Perry, Pauline. "Prospects Poor for Women." *Times Higher Education Supplement*, 6 November 1992.

Touchton, Judith; Shavlik, Donna; and Davis, Lynne. *Women in Presidencies: A Descriptive Study of Women College and University Presidents.* Washington, D.C.: American Council on Education, 1993.

Touchton, Judith, and Ingram, Deborah. *Women Presidents in U.S. Colleges and Universities: A 1995 Higher Education Update.* Washington, D.C.: American Council on Education, 1995.

Utley, Alison. "Women Profess to Salary Bias." *Times Higher Education Supplement*, 30 August 1991.

Who's Who 1992. London: A&C Blacks, 1992.

Tessa Blackstone

GOOD FORTUNE COUNTS
by Tessa Blackstone

Baroness Tessa Blackstone is master of Birkbeck College, University of London. She attended Ware Grammar School for Girls before earning B.Sc. and Ph.D. degrees from the London School of Economics and Political Science at the University of London. Her academic background includes visiting fellowships at Harvard University, the University of California at Berkeley, and Melbourne University; and she holds honorary doctorates from the University of Bradford, Bristol Polytechnic, Middlesex University, and the University of Aberdeen and an honorary fellowship from the College of Preceptors. Baroness Blackstone has published numerous books and monographs concerning education and social policy.

In the House of Lords, where she is a Life Peer, she has been the opposition frontbench spokesperson on education and science and foreign affairs and a spokesperson on treasury and on trade and industry. Baroness Blackstone's experience as a radio and television commentator, administrator in local government, and government advisor strengthened her ability to bring Birkbeck College, University of London, from financial crisis to good health, doubling its degree program enrollments and ensuring that its academic reputation is of the highest standing.

When I arrived as a new undergraduate at the London School of Economics, a bit green and, to be frank, without much idea of what a degree in the social sciences entailed, I had no plans for my future career except that I wanted one. I knew that being a housewife, as a woman who stayed at home to look after her family used to be called, would not be fulfilling. I knew that I would want a job even if I had children. Not for one moment had I entertained the idea of becoming an academic. It was only later, after I had finished my first degree and started research for a Ph.D., that this looked like a possibility.

Having been to a typical British girls' grammar school of the 1950s, the London School of Economics was a dramatic change and something of a challenge. I had enjoyed my secondary school. I was adequately educated there, though the teaching was, for the most part, conventional and lacking in imagination, and the extracurricular activities were limited. But I threw myself into acting in school plays, competitive sports (hockey, netball, and tennis), and wrote for the school magazine. The school was single-sex, small, predominantly lower middle and middle class, and almost a hundred percent white. It excelled at nothing, neither was it a terrible failure in what it did. It was cozy, caring, and bourgeois.

By contrast, the London School of Economics (LSE) was radical, cosmopolitan (40% of its students came from overseas), and intellectually challenging. At my secondary school, I had learned how to be disciplined and apply myself; at LSE I learned for the first time how to think critically.

Studying sociology with some economics and a little history, I was excited by the subjects I had chosen. To stay on as a graduate student seemed the obvious route to take. It was not, however, an easy route. I had married and had my first child before graduating. My husband was a graduate student at the time, and we were penniless. I failed initially to get a scholarship and, instead, started part-time lecturing to help make ends meet. We rarely went out and lived a Spartan existence of working, studying, and looking after our son.

Then came my lucky break. With an unfinished Ph.D. and pregnant for the second time, I was offered an academic post at LSE. I started in my new job when my daughter was two weeks old, staggering in to work, absurdly determined to prove that young mothers could be hired without any concessions being made to them. The idea that I might ask to delay starting in the post for a few weeks did not occur to me. Somehow I survived the first two years: preparing and teaching new courses, finishing my dissertation, getting my first article into an academic journal, and looking after my small children.

Slowly things became a little easier. We managed to travel a bit, taking the children, too. In the summer of 1968, we were based in Morgantown, West Virginia, where my husband worked on a federally funded scheme to devise an input-output program for Appalachia. I sat in the library of the University of West Virginia checking the final draft of my thesis and preparing the bibliography. When we had finished our work, we drove from Washington, D.C., to Eugene, Oregon, and from Eugene to Los Angeles in an old station wagon with two children under five in the back. It was a hard slog, but we saw America. Two years later I won a travel scholarship for young academics to spend a summer in Israel, where I studied their educational programs for disadvantaged children and acquired my enduring and deep sympathy for the Palestinians.

By 1972 I had published a couple of books and, with two LSE economists, was working on a third. I had tenure and was enjoying teaching in a steadily growing master's degree program, as well as supervising a number of research students. My colleagues were stimulating, and I enjoyed lunchtime talks in the Senior Common Room with social scientists from outside my own department. But I had itchy feet. Much as I loved the "School," I knew I had to go elsewhere to broaden my experience. Taking unpaid leave, I went first to Harvard as a Visiting Fellow at the Center for Education Policy Research, where I taught a couple of summer school courses and immersed myself in the American debate about equalizing opportunities through schooling. From there I went to a fellowship at a new research institute in London, the Centre for the Study of Social Policy. But I was still unsettled when I returned to LSE a year later.

My chance for a larger and more complete break came after the second general election in 1974 when a Labour government was returned, even though with a tiny majority. Unlike its Conservative predecessor, its members were interested in the links between different areas of social policy: between education and employment, between housing and welfare services, between health and social security. The government's own think tank, the Central

Policy Review Staff, located in the Cabinet Office and with the task of advising the Cabinet across the whole range of government policy, started to work on these links. I was taken on to join the team that was tackling the problems that arose. It was another lucky break. I spent three years at the center of central government, mastering how Whitehall and Westminster worked, as well as learning about new areas of policy — though, of course, as a civil servant and not a politician. I observed cabinet politics from inside the system and greatly widened my network of contacts in the Labour government as well as in the senior civil service. Above all, I learned about the constraints — as well as the possibilities — of power.

When the time came to leave in the autumn of 1978, I was faced with a different decision. Should I take the plunge and leave academia for a permanent position elsewhere in the public sector — either in the civil service or a government agency such as the Schools' Council — or take an even bigger plunge and go into the private sector from which I had received a couple of approaches? Caution got the better of me. I returned to the University of London, though not back to the LSE, going instead to a professional chair at the Institute of Education. There I was the head of a small department that taught only graduate students. I returned to research and publication and learning about university administration. It was immensely satisfying, but a little dull after the Central Policy Review staff. However, beginning in the spring of 1979 the Conservatives were back in power; and I was better off, given my political convictions, away from the malign influence of Margaret Thatcher and her government. I was free to write what I wanted and to broadcast. During this period I gained valuable experience of the media, presenting programs on the arts, education, and the press, as well as appearing on chat shows and more serious political programs. I made two attempts to be selected to stand for Parliament, failing by one vote the second time around.

Whilst still trying to decide whether or not to try again, I was approached and asked to apply for the job of Deputy Education Officer in the Inner London Education Authority (ILEA). The

ILEA was a labor authority, running the school and college system across the 12 Inner London boroughs. It was trying to put into practice some of the things that I had been advocating as a result of my research on education policy. It also represented a new challenge, entailing far more administrative and managerial responsibility than I had had before. It ruled out writing and research and any further attempts to become a member of Parliament. I hesitated. Under pressure to make a decision, I decided to have a go.

It turned out to be a much tougher assignment than I had imagined. With little relevant experience, I was thrown straight into the deep end. On a number of occasions I nearly drowned. I survived through the life belts thrown to me by my colleagues, some of whom were better swimmers, and through my own strength of will not to go under. Almost at the top of a vast bureaucracy, I was responsible for the work of some 700 administrative staff in the branches or departments that reported to me. The elected members, who were responsible for the authority's policies, varied from the most talented and creative local politicians to be found anywhere to ignorant, irresponsible, and self-seeking nonentities.

At the same time, the Conservative government had started a relentless attack, which later turned into a full-scale war, on the Authority for its radical policies and what was perceived as its high spending and low standards. Meanwhile social deprivation was growing in Inner London, and the school system was being tested to its limits. Against the odds, it still achieved many remarkable successes.

My three-and-a-half years there toughened me up and taught me how to be resilient in the face of setbacks and crises. I learned, too, about how to handle resource allocation from a huge budget (just under £1 billion when I left) and a lot about how to pick and chose the right staff, when to delegate, and when to do it myself. It was learning on the job, which was excellent training for almost anything I was likely to do later. In Whitehall, I had learned how national policy is made. At County Hall (the ILEA's headquarters), I learned about the problem of implementing national and local policies. And I reinforced a habit I had already acquired: a willingness to work long hours and enjoy doing so.

However, by the summer of 1986 I had had enough. Although the ILEA had escaped abolition at the same time as the Greater London Council (GLC), it remained vulnerable. Having completed work on the ILEA's restructuring after abolition of the GLC, I was on the lookout for something different. With perfect timing, the post of Master of Birkbeck College, University of London, was advertised and I applied.

Although I was only 44 at the time, young for such an appointment in Britain, and I had neither the experience of being a number-two running an academic institution nor a brilliant international reputation as a scholar to compensate, the mix of experience I had acquired seemed to suit the college's governors. I was appointed, and I was delighted. Birkbeck had always appealed to me because of its commitment to mature part-time students and to research. No other research university dedicated itself to the education of adult students. No other college or polytechnic with many part-time and older students managed to combine this commitment with scholarship and research at a high level.

However, I inherited an institution with a serious financial crisis, doubts about is academic viability because of its small size, an unbalanced student population because of its disproportionate number of postgraduates, and a serious collapse of morale amongst many of its staff. How could they have been anything other than demoralized, because there was talk of closure and a consequent blight on applications from students and funding for research? I had taken on another challenge. However, I knew from the beginning that this was a battle for survival that could be won. There was so much potential there. It also was an institution with a remarkable history going back to the 1820s and a unique role in British higher education. I knew, too, that whilst sentiment would help, it was not enough to guarantee survival.

With the help of colleagues, I devised a rescue plan that involved a commitment to expanding the college considerably, to increasing our income by various means, and, initially at least, to cutting our expenditures. New management structures were needed to streamline decision making and to take into account the harsher climate in which all higher education was operating, with less money and more to do and far tougher requirements to be accountable. A helpful start in devising these new structures was made in the months leading up to my arrival through a committee, which I was invited to join and was therefore party to its recommendations.

Academic institutions do not work when run by dictatorial methods with bullying bureaucrats in support of overbearing vice-chancellors or presidents. But they also do not work without clear structures for making decisions, which avoid time-wasting debates that are inconclusive and consequently frustrating for most of the participants. A well-run academic institution minimizes the amount of time most of its staff needs to spend on administration and facilitates their research and their teaching. At the same time it allows for proper consultation about major academic and financial decisions. Well-run academic institutions also reward success properly and deal with incompetence and failure. Our students are our most valuable asset; and they deserve the best that can be provided, whether they are first-year undergraduates or in their last year completing a Ph.D. Well-run academic institutions also ensure that junior academic staff are not exploited by senior staff, either by being overloaded with teaching or used as research assistants with their contributions unacknowledged. A sense of community should prevail in a context where competition is inevitable and not unhealthy, unless it becomes ruthless.

I have tried in my seven years as the head of Birkbeck to operate on the basis of these principles. I have had superb support from those who have worked with me in managing a unique institution that should always have a special place in the hearts and minds of those who love learning. In this sense, I have been doubly fortunate.

Restoring Birkbeck to financial good health and ensuring that its academic reputation is of the highest standing has been achieved as a result of the dedication and loyalty of its staff and the understanding support of many people in the wider community who are aware of the importance of lifelong learning and the leadership that Birkbeck can offer in this sphere. We have doubled our student numbers studying at degree level; incorporated the University of London's Extra-Mural Department, involving a growing outreach program into the community; widened the areas in which we teach and research; and greatly improved our research rating so that in the overall league table, after the last research assessment exercise, the college came 12th in the list of nearly 100 multi-faculty universities.

In the small part that I have played in this success, I have been helped by the preparation for my role at Birkbeck provided by my previous jobs, as academic, government advisor, and administrator in local government. Whether being a woman has helped or hindered me, I have no idea. I have simply tried my best for an institution of which I am increasingly proud. Of one thing I am certain: Many, many more women could be running universities in Britain and the United States and elsewhere than have yet been given the chance. I have been very fortunate to have had that chance. In the future I hope many more women will share my good fortune.

Paula Pimlott Brownlee

A BRITISH/ AMERICAN JOURNEY
by Paula Pimlott Brownlee

Paula Pimlott Brownlee is the former president of Hollins College, which is located in Virginia. She holds an M.A. (B.A.) degree in chemistry from Somerville College, Oxford University, and a D. Phil. in organic chemistry from Oxford. After a postdoctoral fellowship at the University of Rochester, Dr. Brownlee was a research chemist for the American Cyanamid Company. She joined Rutgers University as a faculty member, later becoming a tenured associate professor and acting dean of Douglass College of Rutgers University. She left to become dean of the faculty of Union College in New York, followed by the presidency of Hollins College for nine years.

Dr. Brownlee became president of the Association of American Colleges and Universities in 1990. She also has served on several boards of trustees and directors, including the University of Rochester, Educational Testing Service (chair, 1992-94), National Humanities Center, American Association for Higher Education (chair, 1983-84), Bell Atlantic of Virginia, and the Association for Religion in Intellectual Life. Dr. Brownlee has received honorary degrees from 14 colleges and universities. She speaks and writes for a wide variety of institutions and organizations, both nationally and internationally. In addition to her work in higher education, she is deeply interested in contemporary education issues involving the sciences and the arts.

Here I sit, faced with the difficult yet seductive task of producing a distillation of my own life on paper. Such an account must be both interesting for others to read and true to my memories and their interpretation. Because most readers will share with me a commitment to and interest in the world of higher education, therefore I shall concentrate on experiences that are most likely to connect with the imagination and aspirations of those readers.

31

My professional work has demanded a constant search for understanding of what best engages contemporary students in their own education. In recent years, I have been particularly focused on *liberal* education. Descriptions of the purposes of a liberal education abound. For me, however, the purpose that stands above all others is to enable learners to make meaning from the expanding human experiences of their lives. I join that search, finding myself still a learner, right alongside our students. I reflect, of course, my own long-held fascination with what it is that I and others seek to know. Why and how do we strive for understanding? What motivates us, what seems worth doing, what satisfies and ultimately fulfills us?

Those age-old questions used to be focused for me on meaning in my own life. Increasingly, however, I find that meaning constructed in the connections with many others and, more tenuously, in the meaning of others' lives that are unconnected with mine.

I currently head up the only national higher education association in the United States that works with its college and university member institutions on improving the undergraduate liberal education of its students. This position seems in some ways to be the culmination of all my earlier professional and personal experiences. I came to this position from the presidency of a member college, Hollins College, where I had served for nine years. Before that, I had held academic deanships at two very different member institutions and had earned academic tenure as a faculty member in chemistry at the first of these.

However, this unremarkable trajectory of an apparently smooth career progression is set in an unusual transatlantic family background. My father was English, my mother American; and I was a cherished only child. I was brought up in England, first traveling to the United States as an adult when I was 25 years old. Of all the multitude of influences on my development, I believe that my continued strong allegiance to two countries and my inherent singularity as an only child are the most profound.

My parents were unusually separated from everything institutional or organizational. Both my parents were artists in London, had never worked by choice in any organization, and somewhat disdained those who did. The individual expression of their own ideas and creativity and their self-disciplined activity were the guiding principles of their strivings, and these principles influenced me deeply from my earliest years.

I was born and brought up in London, and my childhood was dominated by the effects of World War II. On my sixth birthday my mother was making final preparations to take me to New York to safety for "the duration." Two years later, deeply unhappy in America, she finally procured a precious berth back to England on a troop ship. We steamed slowly through the icy, stormy North Atlantic in February. Indeed, two of the ships in our convoy were torpedoed and lost. But, finally, we arrived back in cold, dark, war-torn London. My father was serving in the Royal Air Force, and we moved repeatedly in order to be near him until he was demobilized after the end of the war.

By the time I was 10 years old, I had attended ten different schools, and my parents were sure that my education had been badly fragmented. They then sent me to a fine girls' boarding school, where music and the sciences were particularly good. It is interesting that it is music and the sciences, together with art, that have remained my lifelong affections. For an only child who had moved so much, the boarding school experience, where I could make lifelong friends, provided important stability. The school was a Church of England (Anglican) school, and it was there that I had my first exposure to religious practice of any sort. Exploration of Christian faith became an important activity during my undergraduate years. Later I turned away toward a wistful kind of agnosticism. But later still, I made a gradual and difficult return to faith, continuing now (with much questioning) as a member of the Episcopal Church.

From the age of five, when I announced that I would be an artist, (and I was thrilled to learn from my father: "Then you shall be the fifth generation Pimlott artist!"), I intended to make art my career. But my fascination with science grew — and I was good at it. I dearly loved and respected my chemistry teacher at school, and so I decided to read chemistry at university. I went up to Ox-

33

ford, to Somerville College, ecstatic at the opportunity to be part of that extraordinary university.

Oxford was, for me, everything a student could hope for. While my formal studies were focused on chemistry in all its complexity and depth, the informal life of every Oxford student was expected to be intellectual and exploratory, and the opportunities were matchless. Like most of my friends and acquaintances, I attended the weekly meeting of numerous student clubs — the Alembic (chemistry) Club, the Oxford University Scientific Society (of which I became, in my final year, the president), chamber music groups and an orchestra, religious societies, clubs focused on archaeology, the philosophy of science, Playford dance, and others that I have forgotten. After the meetings, we would adjourn to friends' rooms for coffee and talk. At other times we would go for walks, ending up at a pub for cider or a beer — but always talk, talk, talk. Our talk ranged from current political affairs in Britain and abroad, through our religious beliefs and doubts, to our hobbies, and to the academic interests of the whole range of friends. Of course, we also discussed our friends, our latest love interests, and the Oxford gossip that we picked up. Yet the expectation at Oxford was that we were "junior colleagues and scholars in the making" and, as such, even in our spare time we were to be about the business of discovering how to engage in and enjoy new learning.

The memory of those vigorous, give-and-take conversations remains a key to my vision of what a good liberal education should encompass. However, beyond that memory one set of experiences exemplifies for me a dream of cross-generational community building. One club made available a discussion group around issues in the philosophy of science; and undergraduates, graduate students, and some dons (Oxford faculty members) all participated together. A discussion leader gave a brief paper, and energetic debate ensued.

Now I had never studied this subject; and apart from a bit of earlier random reading I had done in my school library, I knew very little of the field or its best-known scholars. At first I remained totally silent, drinking in the unique experience of hearing dons expressing ideas, disagreeing with each other, even expressing their ignorance. I had never experienced being part of a conversation where the participants were at all levels of "seniority." Even later, I never said very much because of my weak background. Yet those evenings of discussion remain vivid in my memory: 12 or 15 academics of all ages sitting around informally, tea and biscuits to sustain us, engaged deeply with the subject at hand. This is, to my mind, one important means of building real intellectual community.

At the center of the undergraduate learning experience at Oxford lies the famed tutorial. Every single week during a term, the students each have a rigid academic obligation to appear weekly, essay in hand, for their hour-long meeting with their tutor. My own Somerville tutor was no less a famed chemist than Dorothy Crowfoot Hodgkin, who would later win the Nobel Prize in chemistry, but who was already, in the 1950s, a brilliant and internationally known crystallographer. She had a gentle, vague manner that could be swept aside by a sudden, sharp coming to life over an idea or a tentative solution to a problem at hand. Interestingly, however, it was in my first visit to her home, for Sunday tea, that an entirely new range of life possibilities opened up for me.

Until I saw Dorothy Hodgkin in her home, surrounded by three delightful, rough-and-tumble young children and her interesting and attentive husband, it had never really dawned on me that professional women of stature had families of their own. I had never met one before. Suddenly, I saw this eminent, somewhat awe-inspiring woman in a whole new dimension — as a family person, happy in a rather "ordinary" way. Yet neither of her two roles appeared to negate the other.

After my undergraduate years, I was awarded a fellowship to stay on at Oxford, one of very few so privileged, to work for a D. Phil. in organic chemistry. By now, I knew that I wanted to become a research chemist — and, one day, to be married. Over these years I had various men-friends, one or two of whom might have become the lifelong spouse. The problem of combining career and marriage was never far from my mind and was a constant worry, despite the examples at Oxford of the several married women dons. But all the men that *I* knew well appeared completely unready to accommodate the career ambitions of the woman they would marry. I was quite anxious about this, but there were very few peers, even at a college like Somerville with its wonderful history of successful women writers, dons, and teachers, who were ready to talk about something so personal.

I was very unclear about possible options for a long-term career when my research work for the D. Phil. was concluded. A research career required at least a year's postdoctoral research in a "prominent" laboratory, and this was both appealing and relatively easy to arrange. The best organic chemistry laboratories abroad were then considered to be in Switzerland and the United States; and with my part-American family background, it made sense to plan on a year in the United States.

Preparations to go to work at the University of Rochester made me both excited and apprehensive; however, the United States turned out to be very different from the country my mother had described to me all my life. My reception in Rochester was lukewarm, not from my new research supervisor, Stanley Tarbell and his wife, who were most welcoming, but from almost everyone else. I discovered that I had an almost unique identity as an Oxford woman chemist with a doctorate degree, and so I was considered an oddity. The place of women in American higher education at that time was submerged, and this was a new and exceedingly unpleasant discovery. For many months I did not like what I perceived of the United States, of Rochester, of the university, or even of the department. I imagined that they did not particularly like what they saw of me, either!

By this time, I was 25 years old and had no clear sense of my career path or life direction. I wanted to go back to England as soon as my year's commitment was up. The British civil service flew me down to Washington, D.C., for interviews, and then set up a series of interviews in England at different government research laboratories. But the complexion of life can change rapidly if seemingly small changes occur. And thus it happened that I met a young man in the department who was kind and well-liked, played the clarinet and recorders, skied, skated, and liked the outdoors. And so life became a great deal nicer, and the summer trip back to England became a test of whether I could imagine *not* returning to England to live.

Tom and I were married, we worked in industry (which I truly hated), we had three children in quick succession, and for nearly seven years I had no full-time remunerated job. However, those years at home were formative for me in ways of which I was unaware at the time. I believe I was unknowingly changed from being a very individualistic, focused person, to one who learned to juggle many activities at once. I believe that the domestic experience also helped me develop some of the skills that later would prove essential for an academic administrator.

During these seemingly endless years of our offspring's young childhood, I threw myself into activities I could do at home — arts, crafts, gardening, and chemical abstracting for a journal — or with the children — visiting friends, zoos and gardens, and later, museums and art shows — or in the evenings — playing in a very good municipal orchestra and taking an art course or two. For the most part, I was content to stay at home bringing up the children, free of the awful constraints I had felt in my brief stint in industry. Indeed, I kept reminding myself how relieved I was not to have to be working in industry. Yet every six weeks or so I would have a few days of feeling thoroughly disheartened and of wondering where I would ever recapture the joys of intellectual engagement and stimulation that I had so loved at Oxford. But mostly I enjoyed Tom's arrival home each evening, excursions with the family at the weekends and on trips, and the delight of seeing the unfolding personalities and minds of three fascinating little people.

For these years, I was separated from the developments going on in England, except through correspondence with several good Oxford friends and a few relatives. My parents also lived in the

United States, so there was no pressing need to make the difficult and expensive transatlantic journey with three young children. But by happenstance a friend introduced me to a young English woman living in the same town, and immediately I *knew* that here was a person I really wanted to know and count as a friend. Indeed, Freda rapidly became a good friend; and our families have remained close ever since. However, after only a year they returned to England for good, and we all felt the loss. Three years later our family made the first of what became fairly regular trips to England and different European countries; and on every one of these countless trips, we spent time with Freda and her family. This close friendship kept alive my connection with certain developments in Britain. We connected, too, with many former student friends and their growing families. Meanwhile, of course, we had developed many friends in the United States. It seems, as we moved from place to place, we always expanded our circle of friends.

I count these strong ties of friendship in both countries as helping to give me more than one perspective on the possible avenues to making academic or societal progress. Thus I could follow closely the separate blossoming of women's movements in Britain and in the United States. I watched Open University adult degree courses on British television in the 1970s; our children spent days in school experiencing the "open classrooms" five years before the notion arrived in the United States. To this day, I can talk with complete informality with students in school and university in both countries and make comparisons between some of the experiences of the counterparts. For a person to develop as an imaginative professional, I believe that having a perspective from another culture is a significant asset. Just to know, again and again, that there is more than one way to achieve particular ends surely invites more adventurous thinking. My personal transatlantic viewpoint also has shaped my belief in the efficacy for students of international studies and studying abroad.

I have shared my thoughts on my years at home because the pertinence of private life is so undervalued in our society. Today, after many years in the "public" eye pursuing visible goals for the institutions of which I have been a part, I still count my years quietly learning to be part of a new family, to be part of circles of friends in different places, and becoming a thoughtful organizer of our children's learning as absolutely crucial to my maturation.

But the periods of restlessness that arrived every six weeks or so led to my casting about for something remunerative to do outside the home. I wanted merely to earn enough to pay for a little household help as, initially, I had no grand plan for a resumed career. In the late 1960s in suburban Connecticut there were few part-time opportunities for a woman scientist. Also, after more than six years away, I was dubious about my chances of landing any "plum" of a job. This is where my husband's attitude was absolutely crucial. Without his sustained support — even pushing — I simply would not have persisted. There were no industrial jobs to be had, but eventually I landed some part-time university lecturing, which I was sure was not going to be particularly enjoyable.

After only a few weeks, I loved my new dual role. I spent two days at the university, five days at home, and an evening with my orchestra. Two years of that and the university offered me a full-time, tenure-track position. But then Tom heard he was to be transferred to New Jersey. Again without a coherent plan for an unfolding career, I was fortunate in obtaining a full-time university faculty position. Soon after, Tom's career path became less certain as he left his industrial position of 12 years. We were into a vastly more complex balancing act between each of our careers and the needs of our children and their schooling.

We do not think the children were particularly well-educated in their public schools in the various towns and cities where we lived, though they always had some very good teachers each year. They did well, nevertheless; and we like to think that the emphasis we placed on involving them in lots of interesting family activities gave them a needed creative outlet. We all love skiing and camping and our periodic trips abroad and around the Northeast and Canada. We all played various musical instruments and had a basement workshop with arts and crafts space and tools. Tom and I take great pleasure in our family life and the children's growing capacities. Each child is interesting, loving, and contributes so much to our lives.

One day, out of the blue, I received a letter inviting my interest in an academic dean's position at a college of my university. My first thought was, what does a dean do anyway? Curious, I answered the invitation to the interview; and in the end I was persuaded to try the job for a while. I soon discovered that I really loved this work, though I had never toiled so hard in my life and there was a mountain of totally unfamiliar activities for me to learn and master. However, I discovered that I could care in new ways about the total education of students; I could learn about developments in all the scholarly fields; and I could work with faculty on incorporating new work into the curriculum. What might be a rich liberal education for students, whatever might be their backgrounds and their subsequent careers?

Soon after, the university received a new president; and there was massive reorganization of the central administration. I learned about administrative organization, management by objectives, academic politics and its power, and collective bargaining and unionization. I also learned firsthand about student protests and bomb scares, underprepared students, the women's movement and the Equal Rights Amendment, and the power of legal action. I began to learn about associations on the state and national levels and the importance of knowing other academic administrators. We made new friends among faculty and administrators, and I discovered the strength of "networking." My preparation for this spread of activities, I am sure, lay in those previous years with my young family at home. My ease with mathematics and the sciences enabled me to move into new areas of budget setting, administrative model-building, and later, organizational planning. But at the heart, I drew energy from the search for the best education for our students and by enabling faculty to do their best work.

We made our next family move because of a new position for me. I took up an academic deanship at a private college, one that recently had changed from a men's college to become coeducational. The male-dominated administration and faculty provided a fine educational setting but a very competitive one, which was rather isolating for me and, in fact, for each of the few women faculty. Five years later I accepted the presidency of a women's college, where I spent nine very satisfying, challenging years. The community of that campus and the administrative team I was able to put together were amazingly effective in nurturing the educational development of our women students. I believe that for our students there was no institution in the country that could have better educated and developed their capacities. It was a tremendous base from which to work, and I shall always be deeply grateful for that matchless experience.

Nine years in a college presidency is a substantial stretch of time, and the college had been changed over that time. I discerned that I also had changed and matured; but whenever I thought about what might happen after this college presidency, I drew a blank. I did not imagine myself moving to another college, when I so cared for the one I was at. Still, I was reluctant to stay until retirement, which I projected as 9 or 10 years hence. What options lie beyond a college or university presidency?

Just at this time, the Association of American Colleges opened a search for a new president; and I learned that my name had been placed in nomination. Since the mid-1970s, I had kept active with this association, serving on its board and being part of its meetings and some projects; and I greatly respected its work. I accepted the nomination and some months later was very pleased to be invited to fill the position. It is a privilege indeed to spend one's working life devoted to the strengthening of liberal education, in practical ways, on this nation's campuses. Association work is very different from campus life. Its intellectual scope is vast and challenging; there is little "routine" business but a constant need to stay close to the difficult reality of campus life. After the particularly good years in the college presidency, I am happy never to have regretted this last move. Tom continues in university teaching, and we both are stretched by new friends and living circumstances in the Washington, D.C., area.

And so to the present. As I write, I have attained the age of 60; I am grateful for the experiences of my life and I look forward to the unknown future with interest and much zest. In the next few years, Tom and I face another set of life transitions — to be made singly, together, and in conjunction with our now widely-scattered and growing family. I sometimes think about trying a sharp break with my current professional path; art still beckons strongly. It is so encouraging to see that it is indeed by liberal educational values that I, too, have been freed. I believe that despite all the anxieties of these times, the hope for the society in which we live, as well as for my own growing family, abides in educating well — and in the most capacious way imaginable.

Juliet Campbell

THE MISTRESS'S STORY

by Juliet Campbell

Juliet Campbell is mistress of Girton College, Cambridge University. She earned a B.A. degree in Philosophy, Politics, and Economics and an M.A. from Oxford University before embarking on a career in Her Majesty's Diplomatic Service, which took her to Brussels, Bangkok, The Hague, Paris, and Jakarta from 1961 to 1983. Her appointments in the Foreign and Commonwealth Office gave her responsibilities for Western Europe and the European Community, Press Relations, and Training.

After serving as H.M. Ambassador to Luxembourg from 1988 to 1991, Mrs. Campbell assumed the post of Mistress of Girton College, Cambridge. She serves on the University Council as well as being chair of the European Matters Committee, deputy vice chancellor, trustee of the Cambridge European and Overseas Trusts, and a member of other committees related to international connections, management, and public relations. Mrs. Campbell also is a trustee of Changing Faces (a charity for the disfigured), a governor of Queen's College, Harley Street (a girls' secondary school), and a member of the Academic Council of Wilton Park International Conference Center.

I never sought a career in education. Therefore, it is difficult to take myself seriously as a "presidential pioneer" for the purposes of this study. Indeed, it is still something of a surprise to find myself Mistress of Girton and thus the successor of Emily Davies, the true pioneer of higher education for women in Britain.

Emily Davies founded Girton in 1869 as the "college for women," the first college in Cambridge — or any other university in Britain — to admit women. She was determined that her students should have the same education and take the same examinations as the men. This she achieved, and much else besides, because she was a formidable fighter. She met great opposition, not least in Cambridge itself; and it was not until 1948 that Cambridge

University allowed women formally to receive the degrees for which they had been taking the qualifying examinations for more than 70 years.

I arrived at Cambridge in 1992 to a very different situation. Girton itself had gone mixed [coed] more than a decade earlier and the university now has an equal opportunities policy that it takes very seriously. However, women still are a minority of the academic community at all levels; and the higher up you look, the more marked this is.

But let me begin at my own beginnings. The rather unusual circumstances of my childhood have had a lot to do with what followed. I was an "army brat" with a wartime childhood. My first memories are of Palestine, where my father had been sent to help contain Arab/Jewish tension in what was still a territory ruled by the British under a mandate from the League of Nations. Muddled with my memories of olive groves and donkeys and fetes at Government House are more sinister ones of half-heard stories of the murder of British soldiers by the Stern Gang. In 1941, with Rommel advancing across North Africa, the British government evacuated all army dependents from the Middle East. My mother, my two older brothers, and I went to South Africa. Our train was bombed on the way to Suez, and the ship before ours was sunk with great loss of life. One of those drowned was a girl who had been our neighbor in Jerusalem.

The Cape was a new world, prosperous and, to a child at least, free of the tensions of war or the bitterness that apartheid was later to bring. We went to live with friends whose garden had an orchard of loquot trees in which I used to climb. We visited a game reserve and beautiful Cape Dutch houses that remain my ideal of domestic architecture. I went to Herschel, one of the leading girls' schools. Perhaps the oddest feature of this life was that it was a world almost entirely populated with women and children, evacuees whose men were at the Front. My own father appeared briefly once or twice from the Western Desert, Mesopotamia, or somewhere else of which I had vaguely heard. This horde of refugees must have been difficult for South African society to absorb.

In 1944 we went back to England, again in a troop ship, which zigzagged across the Atlantic to avoid the German U-boats. It was great fun, and the crew gave me orange boxes on which to slide around the decks. Then we were in England with doodle-bugs, blackouts, rationing, and a succession of homes, usually other people's. My father went to France with Montgomery's staff, then to Belgium and Germany. In due course I went to boarding school.

In 1949 my family went back to the Middle East, this time to Lebanon, where my father, retired by now from the British Army, had a job with the United Nations trying to settle another lot of refugees, those who had left Palestine on the creation of Israel. Beirut in the early 1950s was a wonderful and exciting city, a mix of East and West. For a couple of years I stayed there from summer to Christmas with a term at the College Protestante Francaise and the other two terms at my long-suffering English boarding school. In some ways I envied girls who grew up with the same friends next door, but most of all I gloried in my times in Lebanon with its splendid mountains and lively cosmopolitan society. I was not unhappy at boarding school in England, but I felt as though I was killing time until I could get back to something more interesting.

This was not an ideal preparation for university entrance examinations; and when the time came, I went to crammers for special coaching, first in London, then in Oxford, with as much time as possible in Beirut in between. I owe it to my mother that I went to university at all. Having missed a proper education herself, she was determined that her daughter should have the best possible opportunities; and being a forceful woman, she got her way. Exams apart, I think my varied experience was as good a start for life at university as any other.

I went to Oxford with unrealistic expectations of joining an intellectual elite. I found my fellow students were much like me. Among them I found friends to last a lifetime. I studied philosophy, politics, and economics and enjoyed my work, regularly doing my stint but not in retrospect really stretching myself. I got my deserts, a good second-class degree. I never seriously considered the possibility of getting a first. Indeed, since I knew myself to be no intellectual, I would have felt it somehow improper to have got one. (However, this is not an attitude I recommend to my students today.)

Then came the question of a job. I remember thinking wistfully how nice it would be to have a vocation. But how lucky we were to have a choice. Looking back, it seems obvious that I should have tried for the Foreign Office. Among those who shared the night-clubbing glamour of Lebanon with me as I was growing up, the brightest stars were the young men of the Foreign Office who were learning Arabic in the mountains above Beirut. I wanted to prove that anything they could do I could do. I also was determined to launch myself on a career, as opposed to the secretarial course that all too many of my friends at Oxford went on to. Of course, I would get married — probably at the age of 24 — but a career would keep my options open. For all that, it was a considerable surprise when the Foreign Office offered me a job, first on a temporary basis, then permanent.

Women were still scarce in the Diplomatic Service in the late 1950s. The Eden reforms opening recruitment to women had been passed a decade earlier, but there was not yet equal pay, and my letter of appointment said that I would have to resign if I got married. (This marriage bar for women lasted until 1972.) It was in many ways a man's world, and my role models were almost all men. I met much courtesy and kindness. I know I was turned down for jobs once or twice because I was a woman, and inevitably I sometimes felt excluded. But I was not looking for discrimination and did not find it. I would have deeply resented any easing of rules or standards in my favor. I wanted to prove myself without concessions. This time I really did feel I was entering an intellectual elite, and I was rather dazzled by it.

My first job was in the Western Department; and in this, as so often afterwards, I was lucky. The department dealt with the Western Alliance as well as Western Europe. It was a time of crisis in Berlin, of the return of de Gaulle in France, of the signature

48

of the Treaty of Rome, which established the European Community (with Britain so disastrously standing aside). For a young diplomat it was a splendid vantage point; and as I struggled to learn the arcane mysteries of handling dispatches, taking records, and drafting departmental letters, I was treated to a crash course in mid-20th century politics very different from what I had studied at Oxford. I also got to know a wide range of people at all levels of the service, something that stood me in great good stead for the rest of my career. I expect it is true in most jobs that it matters whom you know. It certainly did in the Foreign Office in those days and, with no old boy network behind me, it was a real help to start off in a job where I caught the eye of the people who mattered. And one advantage of the scarcity of women was that one was bound to be noticed.

It is difficult to compress a career of more than 30 years into a few paragraphs and to give any sense of what it was all about. This is particularly true of a career that takes one to such different places to carry out what can be very different jobs. A career in the British Diplomatic Service typically is built around three or four areas of specialty. In my case, these were Western Europe as the main theme with Southeast Asia as the minor. I was most involved in political work, often multilateral, with spells of dealing with the press and one of looking after the service's varied training requirements. I served in Bangkok and Jakarta, as well as Paris and all three Benelux countries. I called on hundreds of officials and drafted thousands of reports. During spells in London I gave dozens of press conferences as a Foreign Office spokesperson and sat through all too many Parliamentary debates in the Official Box, the seat where officials lurk silently in case their minister needs help. And I participated in some of the key developments of the European Community. I watched de Gaulle's Foreign Minister Couve de Murville deliver the quietus to Britain's first negotiations for membership in 1963. I celebrated the success of a later attempt with Dutch friends in The Hague in 1972, only to find myself back in London two years later trying to renegotiate the terms of entry following a change of government in

Britain. As ambassador in Luxembourg, I played my part in the negotiation of the controversial Treaty of Maastricht, which converted the European Community into the more ambitious European Union. But that is where my diplomatic career ended and I moved on to a new life in academia.

We all do a lot of living in 30 years, but I think my Foreign Office years marked me in ways that a more static life would not have done. I learned self-reliance the hard way and a determination to stick out the bad patches as well as to enjoy the good. For all the glamour of living in exotic places, one can be very lonely when far from family and friends. I developed an ability to talk to a wide variety of people in very different circumstances, albeit often at a rather superficial level. And, like most civil servants, I became a bit of a pedant about the written word. I also gradually developed a greater confidence in my own sense of values. I was rather surprised to find, when I was put at the head first of a Foreign Office Department and then of an embassy, that I developed quite clear ideas about what I wanted to do and had no particular problems with making decisions. It is often said that women are well suited to be second in command, but in fact I found it much more difficult to second guess how somebody else would tackle any given problem than to work out what I thought I should do myself. I greatly enjoyed having my own embassy and felt that I arrived in Luxembourg with the right skills and experience to do a good job.

If everything was falling into place so nicely, why then did I decide to change course, abandon the diplomatic life, and come to Cambridge? There were, of course, a number of reasons, some personal, some professional. I was due to leave Luxembourg; and with the new family connections I had acquired on marriage, I did not relish the likely prospect of another posting to the far side of the world. Furthermore, I felt that I had achieved what I was likely to in the Diplomatic Service. Girton offered a new and different challenge. If I am honest, I also must admit that I was immensely flattered when the message came to say that the college was minded to elect me as mistress — if I could first reassure them that I would accept the post. (Note the typical Cambridge formulation.) By then I had already become fascinated by what I had learned of the problems of higher education in today's world. When I looked forward to an enjoyable weekend's dither as to how to reply, my husband briskly pointed out that it was clear I had already decided.

Three years later I feel pretty well established in Cambridge. There is still much I do not understand about the arcane way in which this ancient university, which is also at the cutting edge of so much modern scholarship, chooses to govern itself. But the diplomatic trick of learning the essentials fast has stood me in good stead, and I have been able to shape a role for myself that is satisfying and that lets me use my experience constructively. Perhaps I should say two roles, because in this federal structure the affairs of college and central university, though interlocking, are still remarkably separate. In brief, the university sets the syllabus and runs all the exams in addition to providing the large-scale facilities, such as labs and major libraries. It also provides lectures that are open to all members of the university. But it is the colleges that admit students and direct their studies, providing the individual teaching that is the hallmark of the Oxbridge system. Colleges also provide accommodations and the social contexts of university life. Most academics are engaged in a variety of roles at both levels, but college loyalties run very deep.

As elected mistress of an independent college with its own charter from the Privy Council, I have no job description and can be dismissed only if I behave scandalously. I have few formal powers but very considerable influence. This I use as best I can to get the college authorities and, in particular, the governing council to address the issues that I consider important for the continuing success, happiness, and prosperity of the college community. This community consists of some 60 active teachers and researchers and some 650 students, both graduate and undergraduate; and they cover the whole range of subjects taught in the university. It is a lively, friendly, and distinguished academic community with a strong personality of its own.

At university level, too, Cambridge is governed by a system of participative democracy run riot. I quickly found myself sitting on all sorts of university committees, as well as elected to the University Council. Of course, this greatly helped my learning process. I also have been lucky enough to find the right cause needing a champion at the right time: the university's relationship with Europe. This is not the place to expand on the disastrous turn taken by British policy towards Europe over the last few years. Suffice it to say that I believe it is vital to provide the intelligent young people who come through Cambridge with the opportunity to equip themselves to live and work in the developing Europe of which Britain will remain a part. Cambridge has, of course, always been an international university with students from all parts of the world. But it had no coherent policy to respond to the dramatic changes of recent years in both Western and Eastern Europe. Therefore, I was delighted to be made chair of the university's European Committee and have had much satisfaction in working with the academics who are most interested in these matters. A Cambridge European Trust has been established to promote European studies, languages, and academic contracts with Europe at all levels. We are, I believe, at the start of exciting new developments.

It is time to draw the threads together and to consider what advice, if any, I wish to give. There is certainly not much. As I have gone back through my own story, it is clear that nobody setting out to become the head of an academic institution would take the path I took. There was so much chance and luck involved and they were rooted in the times. I was lucky to grow up when the Foreign Office had just opened its doors to women, lucky to marry after the dread marriage bar for women had been rescinded, lucky to have a track record to offer when Girton was looking for a new mistress.

But there are some lessons that apply for professional women, whatever the path taken. I would say to women: Don't underestimate yourself. Don't give up too easily. Seize the chances when they come. Above all, be yourself. You will probably have to come to terms with an institutional culture that presents its own problems. This calls for compromise but not surrender. Do not think you have to be a pseudo-man to succeed in what is still largely a man's world. Do not play power games unless you want to. Interest and enthusiasm are stronger motivators than authority and suit many women better as a leadership style. Try to keep yourself in perspective and not to take it all too seriously. Life is above all for living, and not to enjoy it is a waste. And don't forget Mehitabel: "It's cheerio, my deario, that sees a lady through!"

Carol A. Cartwright

BY THRIVING AND STRIVING, "FIRSTS" ARE SECONDARY
by Carol A. Cartwright

Carol A. Cartwright is the president of Kent State University in Ohio. She earned a B.S. in Early Childhood Education from the University of Wisconsin-Whitewater and M.Ed. and Ph.D. degrees in Special Education from the University of Pittsburgh, after which she served as a Research Fellow at Birkbeck College, University of London, and at Plymouth Polytechnic in England. She has authored and co-authored with her husband numerous books and articles dealing with special education.

Before assuming the presidency of Kent State University, Dr. Cartwright was vice chancellor for academic affairs at the University of California at Davis and dean for undergraduate programs and vice provost of the Pennsylvania State University. She is past chair of the board of the American Association for Higher Education, and she has served on the board of directors of the American Council on Education. She currently serves on the board of the National Association of State Universities and Land-Grant Colleges.

On 11 October 1991, I looked out on what had become the newest of my "families" — the mosaic of Kent State University students and alumni, faculty and staff, trustees and administrators gathered for my inauguration. As I accepted the responsibility of becoming Kent's tenth president, I also recognized how many internal choices and external events had brought our journeys together. I felt a personal bond with Kent that spoke to the risks and responsibilities that we shared, as well as to the timing and circumstances that had brought us together. I knew I was at the right place at the right time.

The institution I was leading had been founded in the first decade of this century as a normal school. It was, nearing the end of this century, a multi-dimensional, nationally recognized research university with worldwide influence in such areas as liquid crystals. And, yes, it would always be the campus where four students were killed on 4 May 1970 during an antiwar rally. And I would always be its first woman president. But, neither Kent nor I had to be frozen in time. Meeting challenges and change head-on allows both of us to get on with the important business of transforming the university for the 21st century. We are both bringing the best and most important aspects of our history forward with us.

Reflecting about significant parts of my own history brings to mind the words of others — words that express personal values, words that have become touchstones. One of my personal heroes is Dr. Lewis Thomas, whose life was truly greater than any of its isolated parts. More than a scientist, a writer, or teacher, he transcended his disciplines to teach and inspire. "We are at our human finest," he has written, "dancing with our minds, when there are more choices than two. Sometimes there are ten, even 20 different ways to do, all but one bound to be wrong, and the richness of the selection in such situations can lift us onto totally new ground."

My own personal search — my own "dancing of the mind" — began when I made a conscious choice to attend college. That choice came more from the influence of my high school experience in Brookfield, Wisconsin, than from my family background. I was the oldest of three children and the only daughter of a father who worked for the railroad and a mother who left her career as an executive secretary to raise her family. I was born in Sioux City, Iowa; and I spent part of my childhood in Kansas City and St. Louis, Missouri, and Tulsa, Oklahoma, before moving to a recently consolidated high school in Brookfield, near Milwaukee. Intellectually, this was an exciting and stimulating time. I was challenged by this new environment that included more privileged students, resulting in a vision of the future that reached far beyond high school.

My parents were not opposed to college, but neither one had experienced it. In order for me to attend college, I had to choose the nearby University of Wisconsin-Milwaukee, live at home, and hold down three part-time jobs. UWM offered me the opportunity to pursue chemical engineering, but the chilly reception I received in 1958 as a student in a primarily male field taught me some important lessons about what happens to a student when there is a less-than-supportive atmosphere.

Over the course of my education I would work in a women's clothing store, as a babysitter, waitress, housecleaner, statistician in a meat packing plant, and as a secretarial replacement at a tannery in order to earn tuition funds. Working was expected, but living at home was a source of disappointment, since the whole idea of college was to go away. Leaving home meant considering both cost and curriculum; and though I would have preferred to stay within the sciences, the $100 more that was needed to study these courses at the university's main campus in Madison could just as easily have been $100,000. Although choosing the University of Wisconsin-Whitewater, the state teachers college, meant a more traditional course in education, it also offered an affordable alternative to a complete college experience — and I took it.

Ironically, part of Kent's challenge as the only residential public university in northeastern Ohio is to help define campus life for our rapidly changing student population. Now, as in earlier days, we are struggling with the issues of access and price. But if we do things right and put our resources behind our students, college will have one more dimension — the quality experience of campus life — during this exciting transition, as it did for me.

At Whitewater, I was actively engaged in campus life, including serving as a staff member and editor of the yearbook. When a young senator by the name of John F. Kennedy visited the campus seeking support for his bid for the presidency, I was one of the student leaders who had an opportunity to meet him. Later, as a new teacher trying to deal with both my own reaction to President Kennedy's assassination as well as comforting a room full of sobbing first-graders, I would recall my brush with history.

That meeting was one of those defining moments that truly inspire. It has helped remind me, as both an educator and a parent, that our students invest more than money and time in a college education. They trust us with their dreams. I feel a special responsibility to help higher education stay in touch with those dreams and to help students reach even deeper — allowing our students to discover, as I did, dreams that they never even imagined.

I also recount this particular part of my life because, without the access of public higher education, my journey would not have been possible. This ability to provide access is one of the greatest strengths of American higher education and one that many believe to be in danger. My first day at Kent was the beginning of a series of major budget reductions in state funding for higher education in Ohio and part of an ominous trend nationwide. It was becoming obvious that the old formula of relying on low tuition, federal grants and loans, and public support simply would not work anymore. Without different financing and new ways of providing services, we will not be able to guarantee access to the next century of dreamers.

New questions about accountability also are being posed as our students and their parents, our communities, and legislators ask us hard questions about how we are managing their universities. Future solutions must take new approaches to solving problems and must incorporate new styles of leadership. Fortunately, my background has prepared me for change.

Armed with an undergraduate degree in early childhood education, in 1962 I found myself as a first-grade teacher in an area exploding in population in suburban Pittsburgh. At one point in the year my classroom included 48 children. Some of them were struggling; and I felt that if I were to make a difference, I needed more education to reach them. Although I had expected to continue teaching while working toward my master's degree part-time in the evenings, one of the professors noticed my work and invited me to apply for a Federal Fellowship at the University of Pittsburgh, which was a private university at that time. I also had been working as a waitress to earn enough extra money for a trip to Europe. Somehow I managed both the trip and applying for and winning the fellowship.

Coming home from a summer trip through Europe to that fellowship meant that, for the first time, I could go to school full-time without working. Though I honestly believed that I soon would be returning to the classroom equipped with the skills needed to teach those students who were having difficulty learning, the more involved I became in research about their problems, the more intrigued I became with the larger role of research and the fascinating, evolving discipline of special education.

At that time, the field of special education was quite different from the shape it has taken today. Terms such as *inclusion* and *mainstreaming* were unheard of. The focus was on a disease model and finding a "cure" for disability. The movement to mainstreaming and to treating youngsters with disabilities as individuals who can and should function in everyday life is quite recent.

I have lived through and helped create some significant changes in my own field. I am quite proud to have made some contributions in my field that are opening young, special minds; but I did not do it alone. The energy from ideas was shared by another intellectually curious doctoral student, Phillip Cartwright, who also became my husband and the father of our three wonderful children. He had come to Pitt from the Institute for Research on Exceptional Children at the University of Illinois, one of the premier programs in special education. We met in the fall of 1964 and married in June 1966, cementing our partnership in work and life. Blending the best of his knowledge about systems and a newly emerging technology with my ability to think about their creative application for special education teaching, we created the first computer-based courses for college students.

Our state-of-the-art computer program was similar to today's multimedia learning environments, but at the time it looked more like Rube Goldberg's technology than IBM's. We were able to develop simulations and tutorials that would help teachers identify and deal with the special needs of children. We were stretching the boundaries of what was considered avant garde then, and the content we were teaching anticipated what four or five years later would become a federal law, the Education for All Handicapped Children Act of 1974. We also anticipated the need for the content to be at the fingertips of teachers in the schools. Delivered exclusively by computer, this course was taken all over the country in a specially constructed semitrailer. Teachers taking the course earned credits from their local schools, and they were provided with a toll-free telephone number so they could talk to "the professor." When their course was completed, the van packed up and moved down the road to the next school. The innovation was in both the approach we took and the content we were teaching. The course is still widely distributed and used at more than 50 colleges and universities in the United States and Canada.

Right out of graduate school, Phillip and I took jobs at the University of Hawaii. Only one year later, Penn State recruited him and I went along. In those days, there was no thought of remaining behind to finish my work. Because "our" work was important, I didn't feel I was giving up anything — merely changing venue. As it turned out, Penn State also created important opportunities for leadership.

It was at Penn State that I also first learned about Kent State University. In 1970, about the time of the shooting at Kent, my husband and his other male colleagues were activated in safety patrols to help maintain calm on our campus. Women were excluded from these responsibilities. Twenty-five years later, I hope it is a sign of our progress that I will be responsible for commemorating that anniversary at Kent.

When I was recruited for positions at the University of California at Davis and also Kent State, my husband moved with me; and his own teaching and consulting work continued to thrive. As a family we have experienced a wide range of attitudes and responses to the approach that was best for us. In the end, we had confidence that decisions we made were best for us, regardless of others' attitudes. Indeed, we have lived through some great changes in personal and institutional attitudes, and I hope that our experiences have made me more sensitive to the issues of dual-career families and the special demands that research-oriented disciplines can place on families. I know that no leader can be effective without learning to anticipate and to live with and through the challenges of change.

Fortunately, I was directed toward the leadership path early in my teaching career when a colleague at Penn State took me aside and said, "You have a gift — you have the ability to take in discussion, live with ambiguity, and build consensus. Don't ever underestimate that gift — use it." I remembered those words while serving on the Penn State Faculty Senate, gaining new perspectives as a member of key policy committees, and then helping to develop strategic issues in the university's long-range plan for the 1980s. As a junior member of that planning task force — almost everyone else was either a vice president or a dean and I was an associate professor — I chaired the group that studied faculty issues while the others reviewed mission, student, and resources issues. I believed then that Penn State felt that having a woman on the task force was important, but I also knew that there were many accomplished women to choose from. From the university's point of view, they wanted someone who had already demonstrated some capacity for managing groups, building consensus, and getting work done. Leading this task force placed me, for the first time, in regular contact with the president, the provost, and the board of trustees. It proved to be important in my preparation for broader leadership.

A short time after the task force had completed its work, I received a call from another participant. He informed me that he thought I probably would be asked to consider administrative positions but assumed that, because I was successful and happy as a faculty member, I might not want a change. However, he did have an offer he hoped I would not refuse. There was an unexpected opening for an acting associate dean. "If you like it, you'll have to compete for this position, but at least you'll know what you're getting into. If you don't like it, at least you will have satisfied yourself about whether or not you should be exploring administration, and we'll be grateful because you will have helped us out in a pinch." I accepted the challenge. It took about five hours to decide that I loved it!

As a visible female role model, I'm often asked for advice about how to be a leader. While I believe that I have a responsibility to respond in helpful ways, I am also quick to point out that the path that my life has taken and the way in which I choose to discharge my responsibilities is a product of my own particular experiences, beliefs, style, and sense of values, met head-on with unique timing. This is certainly not a recipe for anyone else's life. With a clear sense that, finally, we are all individuals, I offer thoughts along the following lines.

I have tried to keep my leadership style direct. My experiences in administration at both Penn State and later at the University of California at Davis showed me that most people appreciate the facts and can deal with the realities of decision making. They want to be "in the know." The key to being an effective leader and communicator is being comfortable with who you are — being confident in yourself and your style. People can then come to depend on and understand the values that form your foundations and the directions you envision.

As for core values, my father was a significant influence in my life. A very tenacious and stubborn man, he simply did not permit failure. To say you could not do something without a serious try at it simply was not allowed. Some people thrive in that kind of an environment and others do not. Fortunately, I am one of the "thrivers," and this has provided a strong frame of reference to value the risks and responsibilities Kent and I seem to have faced alone and together.

A clear sense about personal strengths (and weaknesses) has given me an important sense of security about facing change. My effectiveness increases in an institution with multiple challenges; the more balls in the air, the better. I thrive on complexity and complicated balancing acts and am excited by the challenges and choices that face us in moving beyond our history.

I trust that my leadership has been by example — that I have shown responsibility for making myself available to people who see me as a role model and want to tap into my thinking. Like it or not, because of sheer numbers, or lack of them, women in positions of responsibility are looked at as role models. It is better to accept that reality and use it wisely than to ignore or discount it. I have always been willing to make time to talk to female students about women's issues within the context of their own career interests and professions. While others may have had their own response to the women's movement, my style dictated putting one foot in front of the other in an attempt to get good work done and try to solve the problems that were presented to me. In doing that, I believe I have made some meaningful contributions and some wise and rewarding choices, the most recent being my decision to become the president of Kent State University.

Coming to Kent, I soon recognized the initial attention focused on me as the first woman president of a state college or university in Ohio. Accepting and using that fact to my advantage, I was able to gain a platform to discuss the importance of education and a concern about keeping institutions resilient in the future — at home and around the nation — in light of funding cuts. And speak out I did, logging over 17,000 miles by car in the region in that first year. It was clear I had signed up for two jobs — one on campus and one with the public. Both of them were demanding my full attention because there was a full plate of changes ahead.

As president of Kent State University and as the chair of the board of directors of the American Association of Higher Education, I have developed some specific ideas about contemporary leadership. I agree with Harlan Cleveland, who said that in today's horizontal society, the traditional modes of leadership — recommendations up, orders down — simply will no longer work. He also said that nobody can be fully in charge of anything. I believe him.

Leadership involves creating a process, whether on campus or within a national association, that allows people to get involved in understanding the issues and in thinking about how to solve problems. This process must be coupled with proper timing and organization, and it must have competent and willing participants to achieve results. The leadership gurus have it right when they say that doing the right thing is as important as doing things right. Some of those "right things" include continuing advocacy for adequate funding for higher education, financial support for students, and improving credibility about our results.

We have to be less defensive about accountability. Whether in the classroom or the boardroom, we must be able to answer the hard questions posed by those who support us. And we must make our case better, taking our results to the public, legislature, corporations, and our communities.

We also must expand institutional support to supplement tuition. At Kent a new Founders Scholarship program, a special part of my inauguration, grew to over $2.5 million in less than three years. The outpouring of support from both private and public sources demonstrated that when the goal is sound and the case well made, the support will follow.

We must look toward creating better systems internally to ensure better student outcomes, including decreasing our attrition rates and increasing our commitment to campus diversity. Diversity is an appropriate part of the success equation — not because it is politically correct, but because it is academically sound and economically essential. The faces of our students are changing, and responding to a more inclusive group with a relevant curriculum signals that we are willing to make our learning communities more vital and more reflective of the life around us. It does matter that our students understand and respect the differences they are going to meet in the workforce. And, yes, education can make the difference.

While we must not decrease the vitality of research within our institutions, we must reconsider the role of teaching, particularly on the undergraduate level. Kent has been a vigorous player in that national forum, and our institutional response represents an interesting interplay of leadership and followership. It began when I encouraged members of the Faculty Senate to consider seriously Ernest Boyer's monograph, *Scholarship Reconsidered*; and I included Boyer's thesis about scholarship as a focal point in my inaugural address. Boyer proposes, and I agree, that we urgently need a more inclusive view of what it means to be a scholar; that knowledge is acquired through research, synthesis, practice, and teaching; and that those four categories of scholarship define intellectual functions that are inseparably tied together. I also agree with Boyer's further suggestion that such a vision of scholarship may prove especially useful to faculty as they reflect on the meaning and direction of their professional lives. Our Faculty Senate got excited about what was said and responded by creating a Commission on Scholarship. This has promoted ongoing university-wide discussions that are effecting change from *within* the faculty.

As our resources become more precious, we must continue to seek partners to accomplish together what we can no longer do on our own. We must maximize our resources to serve our stakeholders. This means working together on academic partnerships as well as working with our friends in government and business. Becoming more productive within our universities also means entertaining new perspectives from outside our institutions. By participating in those national studies about transforming the university, such as Kent's recent participation as one of 30 pilot schools in the Pew Higher Education Roundtable project, we can open ourselves up and become a more confident institution. My concern is that, as we try to solve our problems as an institution, we may become too insular. Bringing informed and competent outsiders inside helps us to see ourselves as we are perceived by others. Thus the boundaries of the campus do not become impediments to better communication and meaningful change.

Someone asked me recently if I was sorry that it was not going to be as much fun for the women becoming leaders today because the problems are so great. I thought about it and know that it just is not true. For me, the pleasure will come in the solutions, the fulfillment from the contributions.

In my role as president, I think about leadership tasks and leadership trust. The leadership task for change is to make it clear that people have *permission* to discuss and debate the issues and make recommendations. The leadership trust is that people believe that something will happen when they make proposals and have solutions to problems.

Our goal is higher education, and my goal personally will be to continue the dream that higher education represents in our history. Democracy is based on participation; the ability for full participation is increasingly based on education. It will take both the leadership task and the trust to stay ahead of the changes and sustain the dream.

I will be eager to see where the future leads both Carol Cartwright and Kent State University as they reach out to meet education's challenges.

Martha E. Church

A VIEW FROM ONE PRESIDENTIAL OFFICE

by Martha E. Church

Martha E. Church served as president of Hood College in Frederick, Maryland, from 1975 to 1995. She earned an A.B. from Wellesley College, an M.A. from the University of Pittsburgh, and a Ph.D. in geography from the University of Chicago. In addition to being awarded honorary degrees from nine American colleges and universities, Dr. Church served on the board of directors of the American Association for Higher Education (chair, 1980-81), the board of the American Council on Education (vice chair, 1978-79), and the board of trustees of the Carnegie Foundation for the Advancement of Teaching (chair, 1992-94).

Dr. Church's membership on the board of trustees of the National Geographic Society and its executive committee complements her scholarly achievements as a published geographer as well as her avocational pursuits as a mountaineer in Nepal and Tibet. In July 1995 Dr. Church assumed the position of senior scholar at the Carnegie Foundation.

In earlier days, college presidents appeared to do far more than any one of us could possibly imagine doing today. An article written by Dr. Cora E. Lutz, professor emerita of Latin at Wilson College and, in retirement, a cataloguer of medieval manuscripts in the Beinecke Rare Book and Manuscript Library at Yale University, suggests:

> Few college presidents have ever had greater or more varied responsibilities or undertaken a wider range of related activities than Ezra Stiles when he was President of Yale College. In addition to his manifold administrative tasks, he taught Hebrew to all of the students and was Professor of Ecclesiastical History. Besides these regular appointments, he often gave lectures on optics, astronomy, mathematics,

geography, natural philosophy, and other subjects. As a lawyer, he had numerous obligations to the College, the community, and the state; as a minister, he often preached in the College chapel and in various churches, and performed other pastoral duties. For the students, he served as chief examiner of the entering classes and as judge of their competence for promotion and graduation. Between the discharge of these functions and his frequent journeys throughout Connecticut and into Massachusetts and New York, he somehow found time to read a great number of books: in his diary, he mentions Tertullian, Josephus, Eusebius, Clement of Alexandria, and Justin Martyr, as well as contemporary books in every field, including Mary Wollstonecraft's recently published *Rights of Women.*

I cannot claim to have performed on a par with President Stiles, but I know I would have enjoyed comparing notes with him on the many roles of a college president, as there *are* many — and they vary day by day.

When I attended Wellesley College and got to know its president, Dr. Margaret Clapp, I did not realize that she was a member of an endangered species. As one of five or six lay women presidents among 2,000 or so college and university presidents, she served with great distinction at a college that has had only woman presidents. Although "role models" had not yet been identified as important influences on the young, she was a role model for me not only when I was an undergraduate but also later on, when I was a young faculty member at Wellesley.

My career, which culminated in the presidency of Hood College from 1975-95, reflects my philosophy of women helping women and my deep commitment to the educational needs of women of varying ages and backgrounds. From 1971 to 1975 my work for the Middle States Association Commission on Higher Education showed me how much still needed to be done to open doors for women in higher education. After visiting and working with more than 100 colleges and universities in the Middle Atlantic region, it was evident to me in the mid-1970s that only at women's colleges could women expect to move in significant numbers to the upper professorial ranks and into top administrative positions. A breakthrough on the necessity of requiring four years in residence at a college for a degree was forced by questions raised by servicemen and servicewomen who were accumulating credit toward degrees on military bases worldwide, and urged by such higher education leaders as K. Patricia Cross and Cyril Houle. A renewed focus on careers for women and questions related to residency helped to forge new visions of educational leadership for many institutions, but especially at women's colleges, which were beginning to welcome not only adult students but also women presidents.

Because I had had the good fortune to be a part of the leadership of this movement to recognize and serve adult students while I was at Middle States, I was highly visible in the mid-1970s as a potential candidate for a college presidency. Thus my route to Hood College was mostly traditional — albeit partly unconventional, given my role in working with such non-traditional institutions as Empire State College of the State University of New York and Edison State College in New Jersey, while I was a staff member for Middle States.

The early 1970s were both troubling and exciting years to be involved in higher education. Given Hood's decision at that time to welcome local commuting students, who were for the most part adult women, I felt welcome at the college and saw a good match between my commitments and those of Hood. Nevertheless, there were concerns at the college and elsewhere about whether or not women presidents could handle budgets or raise substantial sums of money, because of our lack of previous experience in these areas. And, perhaps unsurprisingly, some students appeared to prefer father figures.

Throughout my studies and, indeed, throughout my entire career, a number of remarkable women and men helped me, thereby convincing me of the importance of women helping women and also of men helping women and women helping men. I remain in touch with many of those who helped me along the way to Hood and into leadership positions for a number of higher education's major organizations, including the American Association for Higher Education (AAHE), the Fund for the Improvement of Postsecondary Education (FIPSE) board of advisors, the American Council on Education (ACE), and most recently the Carnegie Foundation for the Advancement of Teaching. Of necessity, my closest friendships are with those *not* where I currently serve but where I have served or have been involved in leadership responsibilities.

Over the years I have come to believe that I serve best — and the institution is best served — when I keep the following tenets in mind:

- Passionate belief in the enterprise and ability to articulate that belief among many constituencies;
- Belief in people as colleagues not to be manipulated;
- Preference for discussion and sharing information instead of confrontation;
- Belief in delegation with no "end runs" permitted (in other words, clear-cut delineation of tasks delegated and use of an orchestra model of governance);
- Some faith in modified management by objectives;
- Commitment to making decisions as soon as enough information is in hand;
- Commitment to fair and scrupulously honest interactions on every level; willingness to be candid;
- Willingness to hear criticism and to act on it where appropriate;
- Desire not to use a position to gain another one, as a stepping stone, with no real commitment to the current position;
- Recognition of the need to look ahead and to think globally;
- Belief in the importance of idea dropping and of not having to claim fame or recognition for what others eventually claim of your ideas as theirs;
- Recognition that time must be carefully organized and that being late steals time from others;

- Willingness to give nearly total commitment to the needs of the institution — in other words, long hours and hard work; but
- Willingness to take time off for rest, renewal, and maintenance of a balanced perspective; and
- Recognizing when it is time to leave.

Following these tenets faithfully means loneliness at the top, a recognition that one is serving as a role model for some, and acceptance of the importance of making timely decisions. However, there are times when I feel as though I have a firm grip on a steering wheel that is not connected to anything.

From whence have these beliefs come? The youngest of three children and the only girl, I had the good fortune to be born into a family of active, college-educated volunteers. My mother was the president of the Wellesley College Alumnae Association from 1929 to 1931. I arrived in 1930. My father graduated as a civil engineer from Rensselaer Polytechnic Institute in 1911 and moved from Western New York to Pittsburgh, Pennsylvania, shortly thereafter. On my mother's side of the family, the Boyer roots go back into the 1790s in Western Pennsylvania. On my father's side, the Church roots go back to John Alden and Priscilla Mullins, as well as to Elder and his son Love Brewster, all of Mayflower fame. From both sides came a fierce commitment to family, to education, to the Presbyterian Church, and to volunteer service. Thus as I was preparing for college, I did a lot of volunteer work and expected to teach history at the secondary level.

Educated in Pittsburgh's public schools, I benefited greatly from the guidance of several extraordinary women teachers with whom I stayed in touch until their deaths. As I grew up, I realized that Pittsburgh's churches, social agencies, and hospitals were actively supported by men and women volunteers. It appeared to me that virtually all the women who were active were graduates of women's colleges, thereby solidifying my choice of Wellesley College. Scouting, camping, volunteering, and participating in Peabody High School's Leaders Club and Latin Club were very important to me.

At Wellesley College, I became far more confident about my academic abilities and my capacity for leadership. The most important change in my life came while I was a freshman in a geography class taught by Dr. Margaret Parker, a University of Chicago product and the author of the prize-winning *Lowell: An Industrial Study*. Terribly crippled by arthritis, Professor Parker never let her physical infirmities curtail her love of and enthusiasm for geography. She encouraged me to set my sights high and to consider teaching at the college level, which I went on to do.

While I was an undergraduate at Wellesley, I had the good fortune to know two of its distinguished women presidents: Mildred McAfee Horton, who commanded the WAVES (women in the U.S. Navy), and Margaret Clapp, a Pulitzer Prize winner for her biography, *John Bigelow: Forgotten First Citizen*. I looked on both of them as mentors and received, in return, genuine encouragement as my career in higher education unfolded. Each taught me important lessons about leadership. I remain in touch to this day both with Mrs. Horton and with the late Miss Clapp's niece.

The women's network in geography was extraordinary to witness. My first full-time teaching position came as the result of a telephone call from the chair of the Geology and Geography Department at Mount Holyoke College to the senior geography professor, Zoe Thralls, at the University of Pittsburgh. During my four years at Mount Holyoke, the academic dean, Meribeth E. Cameron, took note of me and asked me to be chief advisor to the Class of 1960, my very first taste of academic administration. Dean Cameron made it clear to me that the Ph.D. was a necessity and that the University of Chicago was the logical institution to attend. A Society of Woman Geographers' Fellowship eased the way. Professor Gilbert F. White, former president of Haverford College and then chair of the Geography Department at Chicago, became my first male mentor.

This past year, I rejoiced in seeing Professor White at national meetings that were presided over by a former student of mine whom Gilbert White admitted to Chicago, even though the student lacked a bachelor's degree. What a profound influence Gilbert White had and still has on both of us. I saw risk-taking in action on Gilbert's part, as well as his vision and commitment to scholarship and service. The fact that I am active today both in the Association of American Geographers and in the National Geographic Society as a trustee I attribute to the strength of Gilbert White's personality and my great respect for his advice whenever it was quietly, yet forcefully, offered. His passionate belief in the enterprise of geography knows no bounds; his belief in people is extraordinary.

The call to serve as a faculty member at Wellesley College came from Dean Ella Keats Whiting in 1958. To my good fortune, an American Association of University Women (AAUW) Fellowship permitted me to complete my dissertation while at Wellesley. With the Ph.D. came a promotion to assistant professor in 1960 and considerable attention on the part of President Margaret Clapp, who made it clear to me she was grooming me for an administrative position at Wellesley.

A Wellesley colleague who was a trustee of Wilson College nominated me for the deanship there, with the result being that I served as dean of the college and professor of geography at Wilson from 1965 to 1971. I loved teaching, and I enjoyed most aspects of administration. My visibility as one of a limited number of female academic deans led to my appointment as a member of the Commission on Higher Education of the Middle States Association of Colleges and Schools. I remember attending meetings of both the American Council on Education and the American Conference of Academic Deans and noticing how few women there were in higher education and administration in the early 1970s. Middle States Commission reports confirmed this dearth.

My first risk-taking of sizable proportion occurred when I accepted an offer in 1971 to be the first woman staff member of a regional accrediting body, the Middle States Commission. Even though I was leaving a college campus environment, I viewed my new role as a tremendous learning opportunity, which turned out to be an understatement as the next four years unfolded. Indeed, I had the good fortune to be with the Middle States Commission

as it was learning how to accredit nontraditional institutions —
with most of that responsibility assigned to me. My work with the
State University of New York's Empire State College introduced
me to SUNY's chancellor, Dr. Ernest L. Boyer, later President of
the Carnegie Foundation for the Advancement of Teaching, the
board of which I currently chair. In fact, on the day Hood College
offered me its presidency, Ernest Boyer invited me to be provost
for undergraduate academic programs for the SUNY system.
Although I rejected his offer, we became colleagues and cru-
saders for educational ideals we both cherished.

When Empire State College was accredited, the American Association for Higher Education exhibited interest in what the
team was like and what criteria it applied. Since I constructed the
team, which included Alexander (Sandy) Astin, K. Patricia Cross,
and others, I organized a session at the 1972 AAHE national conference. Most gratifyingly, the session was packed. In the
process, I met Morris Keeton, Russ Edgerton, Virginia Smith,
Carol Stoel, Alison Bernstein, M. Elizabeth (Lee) Tidball, and
many others who have become good friends. Also, in the process,
I realized that AAHE really was committed to the advancement
of higher education and that ideas worth absorbing were freely
exchanged at its meetings.

While at the Middle States Commission from 1971 to 1975, I
became painfully aware that there were virtually no women in the
senior ranks of faculty, nor were there many women in higher-
level administrative positions. In addition, I recognized ineptness
on the part of some presidents, thereby giving me the notion that
I could be no worse and that I might possibly be better at the job
than some of those individuals. Simultaneously, women's colleges headed by male presidents were beginning to consider female candidates when there were vacancies to be filled. My high
level of visibility in the accrediting world sparked some interest
in the part of several boards of trustees to review my credentials.
But as number two in searches — or even number one in the eyes
of the faculty (Stephens College) — I was not convinced that a
presidency lay in my future.

76

Two people changed that perception: M. Elizabeth (Lee) Tidball, a Hood College trustee, and Donna Shavlik in the Office on Women in Higher Education at the American Council on Education. In short, I discovered I had a network of supporters. Both reached out during an AAHE meeting in Chicago and transformed my life. Lee Tidball assured me that the Hood search in 1975 was open, competitive, and comfortable with the thought of considering women candidates. As I entered my 20th and final year at Hood College in 1995 — and as I cherish the Hood-based Tidball Center for the Study of Educational Environments — I could look back on this advice with some wonder; and I am deeply grateful to Donna and Lee, who reached out to me in a time of considerable discouragement.

What lessons have I learned? I know how important it is to do one's job well and with enthusiasm. Writing and speaking skills must continually be honed. The value of networks is obvious, both to the user and to the one helping. The importance of keeping these connections alive cannot be overemphasized. Notes, holiday cards, postcards, telephone calls, and face-to-face encounters are all important forms of communication.

In light of my early years, I have always volunteered my time to the local Chamber of Commerce and the United Way, to the state as a member of several important commissions and task forces, and to the nation as a member of the HEW (Health, Education and Welfare) board and as a member of the Secretary of the Navy's Advisory Board on Education and Training (SABET). When appropriate, I have volunteered for AAUW, ACE, AAHE, Association of American Colleges and Universities (Dana Awards), National Association of Independent Colleges and Universities (NAICU), and the Education Commission of the States. In return, I have had the honor of chairing AAHE, being vice chair of ACE, a member of NAICU's Executive Committee, and a member of AAUW's Centennial Planning Committee. Currently, I chair the Carnegie Foundation Board and the Audit Review Committee of the National Geographic Society.

As a woman, I have been alert to spot and correct inequities and to suggest not doing something because of the message involved, for example, meeting only in states that have ratified the Equal Rights Amendment. I have tried to make Hood "user friendly to women." Some of my decisions have involved taking considerable risks; other decisions have prompted anger on the part of some individuals.

As an educator, I have worked hard to stay current or ahead of many in the field of emerging education issues. I read widely; and I have several well-known areas of expertise, including the education of women, adult learning trends, and accreditation.

As an individual, I try to be cheerful; and I will always make the best of most situations. A sense of humor is a must. In addition, I have made it a point to develop and maintain interests outside higher education. Being single, I enjoy the families of my two brothers and maintain many friendships made while working in earlier positions. I am learning the game of golf. Of tremendous importance to me is my love of hiking and travel. I have been able to travel to China, Tibet, Nepal, Antarctica, Western Europe, the Middle East, South Asia, and other areas of the world. Getting to know well one Sherpa family from the Everest area in Nepal has brought numerous rewards, as each of the five youngsters in the family has been in touch with me either face-to-face or through letters. I have returned frequently to the Everest area, I have succeeded in getting above 18,000 feet in elevation, and I expect to return again. The lure is ever present; so, too, are the many books to read on climbing Everest. I collect early travel accounts to Tibet and Nepal. In addition, I enjoy photography as a hobby.

I have guarded my time and privacy as carefully as possible. I worked hard *not* to be interchangeable with my position. President Church and Hood College were separate entities. Serendipity, networks, hard work, and some luck have served me well over the years. It is important to me that my shoulders remain broad enough for others to use in order to climb higher. The climb is worth the effort.

Ruth Deech

AN OXFORD HISTORY
by Ruth Deech

In 1991, Ruth Deech became the only woman head of a coeducational college, St. Anne's College, in Oxford University. After attending Christ's Hospital (as a boarder at a girls' public school), she attended the London School of Economics and then earned a B.A. Hons. in jurisprudence (followed by an M.A.) from St. Anne's College, Oxford, and an M.A. in contemporary Jewish studies from Brandeis University in Boston. Mrs. Deech was called to the Bar by the Inner Temple in 1967 and subsequently taught law at St. Anne's College and at the Universities of Windsor and York in Canada.

Ruth Deech's teaching and publications deal primarily with constitutional law, public international law, land law, and family law. Her television and other public speaking engagements include the topics of higher education, women, careers, and divorce; and she is responsible for the establishment of the first two daycare centers in Oxford University as well as its first Equal Opportunities Committee. She is chair of the UK Human Fertilisation and Embryology Authority.

St. Anne's College, of which I have been principal since 1991, is one of the 36 colleges making up Oxford University. It has 450 undergraduates and 140 graduates, and all university courses are available to our students, as they are at the other Oxford colleges. It is sometimes difficult for Americans to understand the federal nature of Oxford University; and I find that the situation is made clearer, if not altogether more accurate, by comparing the structure of Oxford University with that of the United States. I am, as it were, governor of one of the states. But my post is mine until I reach the retirement age of 67, and there is virtually no way in which I can be dislodged. The protection offered by this system of tenure gives me a special freedom that I appreciate and enjoy, to do and say anything I want to along the lines of my principles, secure in the knowledge that no retribution can befall me. My views have become more outspoken, my actions bolder, my speeches franker, and my achievements the greater and the better for it, or so I think. Others may very well disagree.

I was elected to my position by my former colleagues, the 35 Fellows who constitute the governing body of this autonomous college. They might have chosen to advertise the post nationally, as they did on the previous occasion, but they decided not to and to elect one of their own number. To be thus elected by one's peers is, in Oxford terms, almost the greatest compliment that can be paid. I am only too aware of it, and the burden it creates also is considerable. My main anxiety is not living up to the Fellows' expectations and not taking care of the troubles that they metaphorically placed on my shoulders in 1991.

When I took up my present post, I was the only woman head of a coeducational college in Oxford. By the end of 1994, there would be five women heading coeducational colleges; but I was the only one at the time, and the college was glad to have maintained its tradition of electing women to the principalship.

St. Anne's College was founded as a women's college in 1879, as part of the Oxford movement of that period for the education of women who were not admitted to the men's colleges of Oxford. The movement produced five women's colleges, of which only one now remains all female. The others have become coeducational, as we did in 1979, a change of which I heartily approve. There is no evidence in Oxford that women's academic achievements are worse in a mixed environment than in an all-female one; on the contrary, they often are better. And in many cases, young women leaving high school do not like to apply to single-sex colleges. I believe that the male leaders of the future will have more respect for the intellect of their women colleagues and an attitude of greater equality in social settings for having studied in close proximity to them, rather than seeing them in the university setting as a separate, protected species. Therefore, I gladly lead a mixed college consisting of equal numbers of men and women in the student body and likewise among the Fellows. In my view, this equal balance produces a healthy atmosphere without the feeling that one sex dominates the other, an allegation often made against other colleges.

My philosophy in leading a mixed college is the one I have consciously or subconsciously followed all my life, namely, to behave as if equality between the sexes prevailed, to ignore barriers that may or may not exist, to forge ahead regardless, never to espouse the "victim mentality," to believe that anything is possible, and to be robust in the face of alleged sexual and religious harassment, always defending my position as a woman and a Jew in fairly blunt terms. I learned this at school, as will be seen. It has worked very well for me and, equally, for others of my generation. Younger women seem to belong to a different species altogether, of a more sensitive and victimized nature; and as I get older, I find their attitude more and more inexplicable and self-defeating.

My job is the equivalent of running a state or a large village. I chair all the St. Anne's committees, and Oxford is a very democratic place. There is little that I can decide on my own without reference to a committee, ranging from the governing body through the education committee, finance committee, establishment committee, library committee, and many others dealing with all aspects of college communal and academic life. I deal with all the correspondence pertaining to the committees and the life of the college, and I am in charge of carrying out the committees' wishes. I am in charge of all hiring and firing (of the latter there is hardly any), which gives me considerable academic influence. We appoint not only Fellows in every subject (the equivalent of American professors), but also junior research fellows (young postdoctoral researchers taking their first steps on the academic ladder, selected from hundreds of applications) and certain administrative staff.

I play no part in the selection of students, for this is left to the Fellows; and any interference on my part would have a counterproductive effect. But it so happens that I also chair the university's policy committee on admission of undergraduates and, therefore, exert a general influence on the nature and breadth of selection. I liaise with our alumni not only for the purpose of fundraising but also to give them and us a sense of shared history, so necessary in an Oxford where the great majority of colleges are 600 or 700 years old and we are only just over 100 years old. This has had the side-effect of raising the profile of the college, and I miss no opportunity to achieve exposure of our name in the media. We are in a competitive market for students, and I believe that we will attract better ones if our name is as widely known and conveys as much character as those of the oldest, most prestigious Oxford colleges. I entertain guests at the college and spend a considerable part of my time on development activities, very minor indeed on the American scale but, nonetheless, important and difficult.

I have acquired these skills without any training, simply by emulation and by an apprenticeship in university politics. When I was elected into my present position, I was vice principal of St. Anne's College, shadowing my predecessor. I believe I was already earmarked, in that I had been approached by two other female colleges to consider putting my name forward to be principal in those places. This is because I was one of the few women to enter and remain in the world of university politics on which I have spent an increasing amount of time in the last ten years. It came about by accident, when I was catapulted from almost total obscurity as a law tutor in a former Oxford women's college to a top university post (senior proctor) that rotates among the colleges. This ancient post, going back many hundreds of years, involves representing all the professors for one year, taking action for them and against them as required, and sitting on every single university committee, as well as attending ceremonies and representing the university.

Unlike many other women, I found that I enjoyed committee work and decided to stay, even though any Oxford academic who spends a great deal of time on administration, as I do, faces the jibe that those who choose to do this are failed academics. Many missions came my way because I was a woman (childcare, health, welfare, and equal opportunities), not all of which were to my taste. But, as so often before in my life, I concluded that if I did not tackle these things, nobody else would. I seem to lack the usual female fear of committees and realized that the virtue of the university's overly democratic process is that a good case is bound to win in the end, no matter how much it is disliked subjectively by members of the committee, daycare being a good example. It also is a help on committees to speak up and speak out. I remain intensely irritated by women who waste their places on committees by sitting and simpering silently. I am blessed with a loud, clear voice and a direct, relatively concise way of saying things, which happens to be the most effective method of communication on Oxford committees.

In my ten years in university politics as an elected member of the Hebdomadal Council, I have been responsible for setting up the first two daycare centers ever available in Oxford University, in response to the overwhelming and almost tragic lack of such provision. When my own daughter was born, I was able to place her in one of the minuscule number of full-time day nurseries in Oxford, a facility for which I have always been grateful and to which I owe a great deal. Once the topic was brought into the open, the need expressed by young women in Oxford, especially scientists, was irresistible. The childcare battle, however, proved the most painful and difficult thing I have ever done. Maybe I was naive in underestimating the hostility and fear expressed by working men and "homemakers" to this project.

I also initiated the first Equal Opportunities Committee in Oxford, modeled on the United Kingdom's statutory Equal Opportunities Commission. Given that Oxford works so much by committees, it seemed to me that yet another committee was the right way to channel and resolve the frustrations and unhappiness experienced by women in the university. And better to do it through committees than by cliques and lobbies. This has not made me very popular with the feminists in Oxford, because I remain opposed to gender studies for reasons I find it hard to articulate (marginalization, softness?); and I also think that the sexual harassment movement has gone much too far. I have opposed special disciplinary provisions for sexual harassment right from the start. And although I lost this particular battle, I remain firmly of the opinion that sexual harassment disciplinary procedures are not the way to resolve intimate disagreements between men and women or attempted rape. On the one hand, university officials should not be interfering in the affairs of young adults; on the other hand, an attempted criminal act should be dealt with by the police. In this, I am a follower of the smaller group of women who believe that sexual harassment codes do women no good, in that they represent them as sensitive, prudish, obsessed with protection, vengeful, humorless, and totally inept in dealing with men. I am unrepentant.

From 1970 until 1991, I was a law professor (American terminology) at Oxford University, based at St. Anne's College, with a heavy load of students, caused by our system of "tutorials," in which students are taught two-by-two as the main method of instruction, rather than in large classes. I taught property law, constitutional law, international law, and, above all, family law, which I love for its emphasis on human relationships and the interplay between law and real life. I resisted taking up this specialty when first appointed, because it was expected that a woman should do it; but, again, I found that it was something that I appreciated. I miss it very much now that my time is taken up almost wholly with administration instead of academic activities. I wrote many articles on family law and like to think that I influenced generations of students by getting them to think about the subject in a free and often politically incorrect way.

The greatest frustration of my teaching years was that familiar female complaint, lack of time. I have never felt that I have published as much as I should, because I have not had the long uninterrupted days to devote to research and writing, as I have seen my male colleagues enjoy. My greatest regret to date is inability to write a book, as opposed to short articles. This frustration colors my attitude towards equality of opportunity. I will always prefer practical improvements and improved facilities for women over codes and statements of principle. It seems to me that providing daycare, keeping libraries open longer, and ensuring that women have word processors, secretaries, and sabbaticals is more valuable than a code on sexual harassment.

My time was short because I have a family, albeit a small one. My daughter, Sarah, was born in 1974 after a difficult pregnancy involving several months in hospital which, together with the problems of childcare, persuaded me that one child was enough. In this I was, regrettably, wrong. Within weeks my daughter went to the college nursery; and I returned to work exhausted but determined to prove that it could be done. Fortunately, I am strong, because I was managing a more than full-time job with virtually no help at home and a husband who was then in the middle of changing careers and needed peace and quiet to study before giving up his secure job for a new start. The early 1970s really were the worst period, but even in retrospect I can see no other way that I could have handled things.

When asked to participate in the ongoing and sometimes competitive and jealous debate about work and childcare, I say that each woman must choose her path for herself and not feel guilty, even though as a working mother she will be subtly undermined by her "homemaker" friends and, no doubt, *mutatis mutandis*. I believe I was a reasonably good mother, given the time constraints, even though "quality time" had not yet been heard of. Sarah was a very good daughter, which made it easier; and only recently has she begun to look back on her childhood and reflect. I reacted against my own mother giving up her career, as women had to in those days, to bring me up. And I noted, when I was very young, her resentment at her inability to pursue a career. It may be that my own daughter will react against me and decide to stay at home with her own children in due course. I remember my mother pointing out to me constantly that she had "given up everything for me," and therefore I had to achieve something to compensate for this. At a very young age, I decided that there was no point in generation after generation of women "giving up everything" if their daughters were not going to use to the full the benefits they had received from their education. This reflection influenced me considerably, as did my mother's other observation that "my face was not my fortune" and that it was unlikely that any man would want to marry me and keep me in luxury in return for my looks. So it proved. I have always felt the necessity not only to earn my keep and be independent but to establish my worth. If I did not have the career that I do, I doubt whether I would be described by any of my friends in the terms so often reserved for women who have had no careers: a good homemaker, a good cook, a good mother, lovely, talented, athletic, life and soul of the party — none of those apply to me. I am almost entirely what my career is and has made me.

This need to justify my existence also expresses itself in a certain driven quality to all my actions, an insistence on entertaining, doing what is required of the wife of a lawyer, trying to fit in other activities, and leaving myself with no free time at all. The stress of a high-level position, such as principal of a college, is compounded by not having a wife. Male heads of colleges implicitly rely on their wives, who arrange much of the entertaining, give some pastoral attention to staff and students, and arrange the home. All of those things I have to do for myself; and this has left me possibly unable to enjoy free time, even if I could find it. Such hobbies as I used to have have fallen away. My only real outlets are reading and traveling, and even they are very often career-oriented activities.

I would guess that this is rooted in the position of my parents. My father was a refugee from Austria who arrived penniless in London in 1939, bereft of job (he had been a journalist), position, home, and family, many of whom perished in the Holocaust or were traumatically uprooted. An amiable, scholarly man, he arrived too old ever to become truly anglicized or to transmute his professional qualification as a lawyer into an English one. To the end of his days, his English was not very good and his salary as a freelance journalist and member of the World Jewish Congress never very high. He met my mother, who was born in Scotland, when she came to his office seeking help for the emigration of her mother from Poland. It was by then too late, and her mother and many others of her family also perished in concentration camps. This knowledge permeated my childhood, along with a relatively modest standard of living and a sense all round of dashed hopes, lost lives, and the need to make up for it all. I feel to this day that it is incumbent on me to make up as fast as I can for all that was lost by my family in the Second World War. One of my greatest regrets is that both parents had died by the time I was elected principal of the college, an achievement that I would have liked to have offered up to them as the ultimate compensation. They may well be aware of it.

An only child, at the age of ten I was very suddenly removed from my over-protective mother and sent to boarding school, a famous English "public" school to which I had, almost by accident, won a scholarship as a byproduct of taking a national examination when I was nine. The school was another great influence on my life. Looking back on it, I can see that, although it made me intensely miserable, I put that experience to very good use, as I have done many others. In some ways I have cannibalized my previous experiences and made use of them all, however unlikely, in reaching and achieving my present position. Nothing has gone to waste; and this is advice that I would offer others, namely, that most of life's experiences can be built on. Boarding in a school that behaved as if it were functioning in the 1930s gave me some resilience and insight into the English way of thinking, though the academic level was not very high. Many survivors of British public schools would say that, after eight years in such a school, no army or prison camp would hold many terrors. In this I concur. We were drilled, we were made to eat whatever was put before us, we prayed, we played hockey in all weathers, and we wore the school uniform from the underwear out, almost regardless of fit. Nevertheless, I am happy to report that one of the other female heads of college at Oxford also was a product of the same school, and this can be no coincidence.

With a great deal of effort and several attempts, I reached Oxford University in 1962, where I studied law for three years. Oxford was a liberating experience, a place where I could throw off the restraining factors of my childhood and explore new worlds. I made many close friends, most of whom are still my husband's and my closest friends today. This prompts me to comment also that one of the greatest benefits of college education is the friends that one makes, in fact, more important than other activities or even the nature of courses taken. I achieved a first-class degree at the end of the three years and for the very first time realized that I was good at law.

I spent one year at Brandeis University in Boston after I left Oxford, largely because I wanted to go away and also because I wanted to learn more about my religion, a side of my education that had been largely neglected. While Brandeis was not to my taste, the general American experience was an educative one and left me with admiration for the open and meritocratic nature of American society. There it did not seem to matter what one's name was or who one's parents were. When I came back, I qualified for the bar, though I never practiced. I spent three months trying it out, but realized that I would become too involved with my clients, who were all going through divorce, and that the work in the end centered on their alimony and property. I felt then and still feel that progress at the English bar is affected to a large extent by conformity.

Two years spent teaching in Canada in the late 1960s gave me valuable teaching experience and, together with my husband, enabled us to build up the resources necessary to purchase our first home. We have always cooperated financially, and it has certainly been easier and more pleasant to carry out my duties knowing that I can rely on the much greater financial resources of my husband. Together we enjoy entertaining guests and going out to meet other people. The capacity and stamina to mingle socially is extremely important in progress to the top. One can never be too hostile towards those whose company one has enjoyed socially, and many a problem has been solved and an advance planned by networking around the dinner table. Despite the drain on time and energy, this is a course I would recommend to others.

I recollect no mentors or role models. I have not noticed being such myself. Although I am frequently asked for help and advice by other women, this relates to their legal and personal problems and not their career progress, though I would be very willing to give advice about career progress. Sometimes it seems as if younger women do not want practical advice about career progress, but prefer to blame the environment for lack of progress. The worst hindrance now is an occasional failure to be taken seriously — as if one had entered the stage from outside and was playing a bit part, soon to exit, while the drama continues with its male players. It would help to look the part (which I do not), for in England the appearance and dress and style appropriate to a leader are essential. If a woman looks too attractive, she is not taken seriously; if, on the other hand, she is not stylish at all, she will not be popular. The trick is to strike a happy medium between the two extremes.

It is lonely at the top in the sense that there are very few with whom one can share one's problems, and even fewer of them are women. The women heads of colleges in Oxford meet relatively frequently and greatly appreciate each others' companionship and counsel. Women outside the university or who do not have paid jobs are precious friends for relaxation but not for the relief of the worries and anxieties caused by the job, which need to be talked through. Here male friends have been invaluable as sounding boards for ideas and formulators of ideas that I have been able to put into practice. In many ways I have had more help from male colleagues than from female ones for reasons I cannot understand.

Public activities are offered to one in considerable number once one has reached a position such as head of a college. Some mistakes have now taught me that I am best advised to stick to public activities in those fields I know very well: education, childcare, the law, and Jewish matters. I have political interests but have learned that British political parties require allegiance to every part of their respective agendas, if an adherent is to rise through the ranks. As usual, I find myself a dissenter on certain points on the agenda of each of the two main parties.

As I am not given to much introspection, I have no recipe for the acquisition and development of leadership style and skill. I have simply followed my instincts and trusted the overwhelming strength of rationality and democracy in Oxford. My personal strengths are resilience, not minding too much if I lose a battle, and being able to take refuge in home from work and vice versa.

I believe I have not yet mastered conflict management, in that there are several situations and setbacks that have been very stressful indeed, especially when I really care about the issues involved. Unlike many of the men in the university administration that I have met, I do indeed passionately care about the issues that I choose to espouse. Being relatively young for the position that I hold, I always console myself with the thought that I will be able to try again in the future to resolve a particular issue — that time is on my side.

My job satisfaction could not be greater, and for this I will always be grateful. Every day is different; every day is exciting. One can see the effects of what one is doing, not only changes in the institution but in the normal and satisfying progress of hundreds of undergraduates, through their careers at college and on out into the world. I can imagine few more fulfilling jobs and am happily amazed that I should have found myself in such a one, reached without conscious plan. Indeed, at no stage did I ever say to myself that my ambition was to be head of a college. At every stage I have done my best and waited to see what would come next.

Mary Maples Dunn

AGAINST
THE TIDE
by Mary Maples Dunn

Mary Maples Dunn was the president of Smith College in North-ampton, Massachusetts, from 1985 until 1995. She received an A.B. degree (Phi Beta Kappa) from the College of William and Mary and M.A. and Ph.D. degrees in history from Bryn Mawr College. After hold-ing the positions of dean of the undergraduate college and professor of history at Bryn Mawr, she became President of Smith College in 1985.

When Dr. Dunn retired from Smith in 1995, she became the Carl and Lily Pforzheimer Foundation Director of the Arthur and Elisabeth Schles-inger Library at Radcliffe. Her numerous awards include a Fulbright fellowship at the University of Edinburgh, an American Council of Learned Societies grant, a National Endowment for the Humanities summer fellowship, the Colonial Dames Award, a Princeton Institute for Advanced Study fellowship, an American Association of University Women fellowship, and honorary degrees from Marietta, Amherst, Laf-ayette, William and Mary, and Haverford Colleges; from Transylvania and Brown Universities; and from the University of Pennsylvania. Her books, articles, and current research deal with women and religion in Colonial America and with William Penn.

I remember with great clarity the first time I announced myself as a professional woman. I was on an airplane in 1955, returning from a year as a Fulbright student at the University of Edinburgh. While at Edinburgh, I attended courses in a rather desultory way, but I also spent a lot of time at the National Library of Scotland calendaring a manuscript collection, the papers of Charles Steuart, the last British Surveyor General of Customs in the American colonies.

An American graduate student, who was staying only a short time in Edinburgh, introduced me to the collection. An ardent researcher, he was disappointed that the Steuart papers, bundled up in an old chest, were not ready for use. I volunteered to arrange them, the curator of manuscripts accepted the offer, and I worked steadily through the winter at the task. It was for me a discovery about doing history with original sources and confirmed me in my decision to go on to graduate school. So when the man in the seat next to mine on that airplane asked me what I did, I said without a moment's hesitation, "I am an historian."

As it turned out, that pleasant fellow was an interesting source for an epiphanic moment. He was Rudi Gernreich, a fashion designer, who rose to fame as the introducer of the topless bathing suit, a liberation movement of sorts for women. And my desire to be a professional historian also was swimming against the tides of the mid-1950s.

In 1955 women were expected to march to the drumbeat of an exclusive commitment to marriage, family, and male ordering of society. This might have been particularly true for me because I was an "army brat," a colonel's daughter. My holidays from college were spent on an army post and in a social whirl — young officers were anxious to join the families of their seniors. But somehow the thought of rising through the ranks to become, myself, a colonel's wife was unsettling to me.

Why didn't I want to conform to the values of the 1950s? It is not an easy question to answer, but at the heart I think are my parents. My father was a staunchly and courageously liberal thinker in a conservative institution that demanded conformity. He supported a fellow officer who was accused of being pro-communist, for example, which was not a safe position at the time. Being an army brat had its less stereotypical side, too. Immediately after World War II my father was sent to China, and the family went along. So I lived for some time in a country in the midst of revolution, where I had a small job, some independence, watched a world crumble, and listened to my father criticize the party in power. It was an extraordinary experience.

My mother, especially, encouraged me. She was deeply satisfied with her role as wife and mother of four — I had three brothers.

But she also had a special regret in her life that she had not gone to a university. She was a bright girl who graduated from high school at 15. She wanted to go on, but she was an only child in a small-town Midwestern family, and her parents, who found it hard to refuse her anything, made her wait. They thought she was much too young to leave home. So she found a job, then a husband, and never did go to the university. For her daughter, therefore, she had a powerful message; and I grew up assuming that I *would* go to college.

My mother treated me and the boys rather even-handedly. We shared all the chores on rotation, so they did dishes and I shoveled and we all learned to cook and clean. She was very permissive, I think, and anything irksome could be put off by a child engrossed in a book. We were rarely punished. Throughout my life I received steady approval and support; and if my parents worried about the paths I chose, they did not let me know. I have a picture of them flanking me when I got my Ph.D. with no sign of settling down in a conventional way — and they are beaming with pride.

Blessed with a supportive family, I look back and see that I made some good choices. Among them were William and Mary and Bryn Mawr. I entered the College of William and Mary in 1950, powerfully attracted by the historic environment I found there. I was at once drawn to what I considered (and still consider) an extremely lively and interesting group of young women, liberal in their politics, outrageous in conversation. An irritated dean of women once told one of us that our group was like soldiers who, when told to start on the right foot, started on the left and destroyed the smooth locomotion of the troop. We wore that criticism like a badge of honor. I also met faculty who recognized my talents, hired me to grade freshmen papers, recommended me for the Fulbright, and encouraged me to go on to graduate school.

I applied to Bryn Mawr, among other graduate schools, because I had been told that Professor Caroline Robbins would be a good person with whom to work on the transatlantic world of the 17th and 18th centuries in which I was interested. I chose Bryn Mawr because it gave me the best stipend. But when I first got there, I thought I had entered a very strange world indeed. I was not sure that I hadn't landed in a comic film made by the Ealing Studios. Caroline Robbins turned out to be a large, tall, very imposing woman who spoke in an elliptical way with an English accent. The chair of the department, Helen Taft Manning (President Taft's daughter, I learned), was an even more formidable woman who habitually wore a hat indoors or out and had a booming voice. They demanded imitation by irreverent students. The gentle graduate dean, Eleanor Bliss, was one of the discoverers of penicillin, but she seemed to find me formidable.

It took little time for me to understand that what was strange was that I was, for the first time in my life, truly in the company of women. Being a child of the army, a very male institution, and educated in a Southern coeducational college, there was nothing to prepare me for these exceedingly powerful women. Certainly there were many men present, but this was a college run by and for women. I came to love this place where the world was turned upside-down. Caroline Robbins was a wonderful, rather eccentric teacher, who gave me a great deal of personal attention, intellectual stimulation, and support in getting fellowships. I finished my degree in a record four years and sent out dozens of job-seeking letters to history departments around the country. This effort was completely unsuccessful, my letters frequently unanswered. Bryn Mawr came to the rescue and offered me part-time work. Within a few years the department requested a permanent position for me, which was granted.

In 1959 I had the great good fortune of meeting the American Colonial historian who soon became my husband, Richard S. Dunn. He also grew up in a family in which the mother had longings for education. Perhaps that had something to do with his desire for a wife who was an equal partner and fellow professional. He has done everything along the way to make that a reality, especially as our children came along and he shared fully in all of the chores of raising a family. When our first was born, I faltered; it still was considered very unnatural to leave children at home and go out to work if you were under no financial necessity for doing so. But

Richard Dunn did not waver and insisted that if I gave up a really good job, teaching excellent students, I might never recoup the loss and never forgive myself.

And Bryn Mawr offered some comfort. The dean, Dorothy Marshall, had two children and regaled me with funny stories about how a working mother managed. Colleagues were going through the same thing — Brunhilde Sismondo Ridgway, now a world-famous authority on Greek vase painting, strode to the library behind a baby carriage; Sandra Berwind, now a professor of English, and I would meet in the ladies room in advanced stages of pregnancy complaining about the flights of stairs to our classrooms. Bryn Mawr gave comfort — but not much in the way of maternity leave. And so Richard taught my classes for a few weeks — an unexpected advantage of being in the same field — and then it was back to work.

Those were exhilarating and difficult years in which Richard and I were being tested and testing ourselves as a couple of working parents who wanted to enjoy family life and also were very ambitious professionally. The issues of the era — civil rights, the women's movement, the anti-war movement — invaded our lives and began to shape the way we understood both past and present. And I began to acquire skills that eventually drew me into a new career in academic administration.

Committee work provided me with my first opportunity to look at the college as a whole, to solve problems in a collegial manner, and even to try my wings as a leader. The 1960s were a period that brought into question traditional ways of doing things. Faculties were fractious and critical, and younger members in particular were anxious to share departmental authority that had for many years been held by chairs who served very long terms, at the discretion of the president. When complaints like these reached the floor of the Bryn Mawr faculty meeting, the faculty decided to create a committee to look into departmental governance. "Participatory democracy" was in the air.

I was elected to serve on that committee, and then the committee elected me its chair. Although the committee was carefully composed to include faculty of all ranks, I was probably the most junior member, without tenure, and perhaps the most vulnerable should the committee fall on its collective face. It never occurred to me that the project was anything except interesting.

We plunged into this work with a right good will and interviewed every member of the faculty. They vented with enthusiasm. By the time we finished, we were privy to every scrap of ill will that existed anywhere on campus, as well as every opinion about what needed to be changed. We proposed a change in governance, a system for electing chairs. I had widened my understanding of the institution, saw what made it tick, and made many new friends.

Presumably the faculty was pleased by the committee's work, because not long afterward I was elected to the presidential search committee that recommended Harris Wofford to the board of trustees. This was another eye-opening experience in which I was invited to share in the exercise of defining the needs of the institution as they could be served by a president and the characteristics of the president we wanted. For the first time I began to look at the institution from the top down and to see the role of the board of trustees in the life of the college.

Another position that I occupied as a faculty member was secretary of the Faculty of Arts and Sciences. I helped prepare agendas for the meetings and undertook the revision of the faculty rules that had become, through the years, a bit messy — repetitive, contradictory because old rules weren't always eliminated when new ones came in, and so on. This was finicky work, but it gave me yet another view of the system.

Like all faculty members, I served on many committees. Some were tedious, some fascinating, some (such as the curriculum committee) intellectually challenging. What I did not understand at the time was that in doing my duty, I was acquiring an education in academic management in what seemed like a secure and comfortable environment.

Moving out of that environment was a shock. Richard and I spent the 1969-70 academic year at a large Midwestern university. Richard had been invited to take a visiting professorship and I was asked to teach in the summer session. When we arrived, I discovered that the very large history department that we were visiting had one tenured female faculty member. A number of highly qualified women, mostly wives, were teaching for peanuts in a university honors program and patronized by colleagues in the history department. About half of the large cadre of graduate students in this department were women, but it was hard for me to figure out what they were being trained for if their own department was so closed to their sex.

When I began to teach, I announced that students could choose to write a mid-term exam or a mid-term paper. Those who wanted to write papers had to come to discuss topics with me. Young women immediately flocked to my office. They did not really want to write papers. They wanted to tell me they had never before had a female professor. (This was an advanced lecture course.) They knew I was married, and they wanted to know if we had children and how we managed home life. It was several weeks before a young man appeared. They, as one confessed, waited to make sure that "I knew my stuff." They wrote papers.

This was a very instructive experience. During the next few years I began to look more and more at the larger community of historians and came to understand that women were not represented in the central places. Especially through my membership in the Berkshire Conference of Women Historians, I met more and more female members of the world of history and saw how many of these colleagues struggled against the indifference and lack of respect they received in the coeducational world.

When the atmosphere of the 1950s and 1960s did not support the kind of professional choice I made, I was able to offset much of that negative climate by choosing a women's world and marrying a strong partner. But now I, too, wanted the respect of the whole company of scholars. That Midwestern university experience got me up on a soapbox, and I began to play a larger role in the Berkshire Conference and the American Historical Association. Thanks largely to the aggressive politics of women historians, the educational impact of the women's movement, the history of women, and younger men like Richard Dunn who took leadership in hiring women when they took their turns as department chairs, the situation of women historians began to change.

At Bryn Mawr, other storm clouds gathered. In the late 1960s and 1970s men's colleges began to become coeducational, calling into question as they did so the meaning and social utility of single-sex education. Haverford College, long a partner to Bryn Mawr, also wanted to become coeducational, a process that required long negotiations over our possible futures together, negotiations in which I was appointed to participate. My once-comfortable environment became a hard testing ground.

The chance to knit these threads together came in 1978 when Mary Patterson McPherson was appointed president of Bryn Mawr. She had been dean of the college and thus immediately had to replace herself. She called me (I was on leave, in Chicago) and asked if I would serve as an interim dean while she thought about the administration she wanted and then embarked on a search. It sounded interesting to me, as I liked Pat and enjoyed working with her on committees; and so I said yes pretty quickly. I loved it and experienced in the work a surge of creativity and pleasure that was unexpectedly powerful. When the search for a dean was unsuccessful and I was asked to stay on, I said yes again.

Working with Pat McPherson was both fun and educational. She took a thoughtful and collegial approach to problems. She involved many people in making decisions and organizing the administration in new ways. Her concern for individuals and her humor always shone through. In her steady delegation of duties to me and in the way she shifted gears from the deanship to her new office, I began to learn what it was like to become a college president.

Another great teacher at Bryn Mawr was Margaret Healy. Peg, as treasurer, was trying to teach us new ideas about financial management and accountability — lessons the academic world was slow to learn. I had certainly never before thought about balancing anything bigger than my checkbook, but Pat and I spent hours with Peg, both of us learning to understand the budget, to see its weaknesses, figuring out how to bring it to balance and, most important, learning to look ahead. Those were invaluable lessons that I later put to serious tests.

I loved my work, my colleagues, and the challenges we were facing together. Then in 1984 a group of people from Smith College came to see me to talk, they said, about the issues facing women's colleges as a preliminary step in their search for a new president. It turned out, of course, that they were looking me over; and they soon asked me to stand as a candidate.

This was problematic. I had spent 30 years at Bryn Mawr, moving from student to faculty member to administrator. My experience was narrow in the sense that it was contained in one institution. Could I make the change to another place? More important, Richard loved his job at the University of Pennsylvania and would not be interested in moving to one of the Five Colleges of western Massachusetts. We would have to commute. But Richard and Pat both urged me to throw my hat in the ring. They were confident that I could do the job; and Pat said — sagely — that commuting would probably save our marriage, because Richard would hate being a full-time presidential husband.

And so I went through the process of being a candidate and was appointed president of Smith College in 1985. I had had good training for this position, but translation to a larger college and community took a lot of adjustment. (Commuting, however, has not been an unbearable burden. We spend every weekend but two together each academic year and all of the breaks and summer terms.)

I found new teachers. Euphemia (Patty) Steffey, the chair of the board of trustees, was a wonderful guiding hand and a loving instructor. She has unerring instincts for the right thing to do. I inherited a good staff. Fran Volkmann, the dean of the faculty, with whom I spent a lot of time, had a splendid grasp of the issues and the players and clear analytical powers and insight, which were tremendously helpful. I like to think that, with their help and that of many other excellent staff members and trustees, I did well.

But no matter how many teachers one has, the resounding reality of a presidency is responsibility. Much can be delegated, and an effective president develops an excellent staff. But the knowledge that final responsibility is of the essence is ever-present in presidential consciousness. There may be no way to understand that except to experience it. Living with it puts a special premium on abilities to make decisions, to avoid personalizing criticism, and to cultivate humility. And I believe that a sense of humor, which essentially is a sense of perspective or the ability to see things in their relative importance when viewed in a large context, is an absolute necessity.

Each position I have held in the academic world has demanded hard work, tough decisions, and accountability. The challenges often have been severe: When is a child sick enough to keep you home? How do you deal with hundreds of students who have taken over the administration building and at the end of a week seem entrenched? How do you find more money for financial aid? How do you define the mission of a women's college and keep enrollments strong? How do you keep the wolf of deferred maintenance from the door?

Dealing with problems such as these has been stimulating, rewarding, and invariably interesting. I have had the gratifying sense that I have grown, that the issues with which I have been involved are important, and that I have made useful contributions. And now I have taken another new step.

I said from the beginning that I would serve as president at Smith for ten years. Those years were up in 1995. I was invited to take on the directorship of the Arthur and Elizabeth Schlesinger Library on the History of Women in America at Radcliffe. Once again I am drawn to history and to administration in a women's world and in a more reflective position — which will most likely be my last. It's a great life; and were I to be called on to live it over, which heaven forfend, I doubt that I would want it to be very different.

Vera King Farris

OVERCOMING RACISM
by Vera King Farris

Vera King Farris is president of the Richard Stockton College of New Jersey. She earned a B.A. magna cum laude *in biology from Tuskegee Institute and M.S. and Ph.D. degrees in zoology/parasitology from the University of Massachusetts. She was professor of biological sciences at the State University of New York at Brockport and Kean College of New Jersey while taking on administration positions, such as dean, vice provost, and vice president for academic affairs.*

Dr. Farris has served as president of the board of trustees of the Middle States Association of Colleges and Schools and is chair-elect (1997 chair) of the American Association of State Colleges and Universities. She has been awarded honorary degrees from Tuskegee University, California State University, Saint Peter's College, Sojourner-Douglass College, Johnson and Wales University, Monmouth College, and Marymount Manhattan College as well as the New York University Presidential Medal and the University of Massachusetts Chancellor's Medal. Dr. Farris has served on the boards of directors of numerous business, civic, and educational organizations, such as Flagstar Corporation, the National Utility Investors Corporation, the National Conference of Christians and Jews, and the American Council on Education.

I remember the first time I saw my mother weep. She was waving good-bye to her youngest child, who as a young teen was leaving by train for Tuskegee Institute, a college 1,000 miles away from home. Our family was miserably poor, and I could not afford the return fare until five years later, at the completion of my bachelor's degree, which I earned on a full academic scholarship. When I recalled that poignant scene years later, my mother claimed it was sun glare that had brought tears to her blind eyes. I knew otherwise.

I was a problem child in elementary school until a wise teacher realized that my acts of fun, which amused my friends but interrupted the class, arose from boredom and lack of intellectual challenge. However, given special assignments in fourth grade and beyond, my creative energies were directed toward such activities as teaching the class about Roman numerals and building model science projects.

Affording a high school education was a luxury in my family and was made possible only by my holding concurrent jobs as a night-time hotel elevator operator and an afternoon receptionist at a school of music. That income enabled me to give my mother $15 per week and to have a few dollars left over for meals, trolley fare, and clothes needed to attend high school.

The helping nature of higher education beckoned me early in life. During my undergraduate years, my admiration and respect were drawn to the fascinating purveyors of scientific knowledge. When I arrived at Tuskegee Institute, home of the renowned Dr. George Washington Carver (1864-1943), I met Dr. Howard P. Carter, Dr. J.H.M. Henderson, and Mrs. Norma Gaillard, all scientists par excellence who, though not as famous as Dr. Carver, were very influential to me. The science faculty at Tuskegee combined the characteristic seriousness of dedicated scientists and teachers with a gift for sharpening the competency of the next generation. They worked with the individual and tried to develop character as well as intellect. On the outside, I probably appeared to be somewhat scruffy, homely, and impoverished. But my test scores and scholarships must have encouraged my teachers to probe beyond my appearance. In fact, Tuskegee asked me to enter a national competition for acceptance into a summer internship program at Oak Ridge National Atomic Energy Laboratory in Tennessee.

I had traveled to a university in Georgia to take the day-long examination, which was interrupted at noon for lunch. Because I was African American, and of course not permitted in the cafeteria, I sat alone outside on the lawn, contemplating the advantage of the other students who were eating lunch. But I was one of the top qualifiers on the exam and consequently spent a summer of research at the Oak Ridge nuclear facility. Although I was deprived of physical nourishment on that occasion, back at Tuskegee the faculty nurtured my spirit and creativity. The love, patience, and time they spent so lavishly on my learning science and research made me want to be like them; and because they had devoted their lives to higher education, that motivated me to investigate a similar pathway.

On joining the professoriate, I moved up through the faculty ranks, but at a somewhat faster pace than was usual. It usually takes six or seven years to earn tenure, but I was able to do so in two years after receiving a tenure-track appointment. I was promoted to full professor only five years after earning tenure — also a shorter than usual amount of time. While carrying out my classroom responsibilities, I received three outstanding teacher awards at the State University of New York (SUNY) at Stony Brook between 1970 and 1972; the SUNY Chancellor's Excellence in Teaching Award presented by Ernest Boyer in 1973; the Alumni Association Award for Excellence in Teaching at SUNY, Brockport, in 1974; and the SUNY Distinguished Teaching Award in 1980. My faculty experience also gave me the opportunity to undertake research, some of which was published in various scientific journals.

Considering administration as a part of my vocation grew out of my years of service in faculty governance. Early in my teaching career I served on and chaired several standing committees of the campus faculty senate. Eventually I was elected chair of an important statewide committee that was given the job of writing the guidelines for the SUNY Educational Opportunity Program. Chairing an active faculty senate committee, especially of a statewide committee, is an excellent training ground for administration, because success in chairing such a committee involves learning an incredible amount of bureaucracy, logistics, politics, compromise strategies, and negotiation. Sometimes these skills are just as important as the knowledge required to fulfill the committee's agenda. In fact, in 1980 the chancellor of the SUNY system bestowed on me a Distinguished Service Award in honor of the creation and implementation of the Institute for Innovative Teaching and Counseling. It was clear to me that my position as chair of the statewide committee that established and developed the Institute for Innovative Teaching and Counseling represented my first major foray into higher education administration. It was during this period that I was offered my first official administrative position, dean of special projects.

For me, the most appealing attribute of higher education administration is the opportunity to get a task accomplished, especially because in our field the goal often is the acquisition or dissemination of knowledge that will continue to improve the lot of humans. The administrative role involves developing processes or policies to ensure that the goal is achieved. The battery of skills and talents necessary to achieve process and policy development include leadership, persuasion, listening, communicating, and team building. I find exercising those needed skills to be appealing.

However, the least appealing aspect of the role of college president is its conspicuousness. The president's daily life takes place in a fish bowl, and the community often makes a sport of watching and commenting on every aspect of it.

I was never fortunate enough to participate in any leadership development programs in preparing for a college presidency. One of the persons who helped me understand higher education administration was Dr. Albert Brown, then president of SUNY at Brockport. He promoted me into three positions, culminating in the acting vice president for instruction and curriculum and associate provost for academic affairs. Further, he often permitted me to serve in acting positions while senior-level administration positions were under search. These assignments in both academic affairs and student services allowed me to see higher education administration from a variety of perspectives. The strategy I employed in the acting roles was to keep a log of my thoughts about the daily activities and to evaluate my accomplishments on a weekly basis to see if I should have made different decisions. I also held regular meetings with the constituents under my purview. In addition to understanding the agenda for the meeting, I tried to determine what factors would motivate the group and what decisions might discourage or paralyze the group. Once these parameters were known, it was usually possible to move rapidly forward to accomplish any specified goal, even in an acting administrative role.

My administrative career has been concentrated in two states, New York and New Jersey. I spent two years in administrative positions at two of the institutions in the SUNY system, eventually advancing to the post of vice provost for academic affairs at one of the institutions. From there I moved to the New Jersey State College System, first as vice president for academic affairs at Kean College for three years, and then on to the presidency at Stockton State College.

Probably the most useful posts in preparing me for a college presidency were the professorship, deanships, and academic vice presidencies that I held, because those roles have the faculty as their primary constituency. Understanding what it means to be a faculty member and how to work with and motivate faculty is an important asset for a college president. My work as a dean served me very well in this regard. The academic vice presidency also was a very important post because it augmented my knowledge of curriculum, personnel, and budgets and because it assisted me in learning to work with other vice presidents and to be sensitive to their constituents.

I became aware of my current presidential position when the previous president of the college told me he planned to resign. Shortly thereafter, several faculty members from Stockton urged me to accept a nomination for the position. Stockton had several viable internal candidates for the presidency, even though the college recently had experienced major power struggles between institutional constituencies and was in the throes of several legal disputes between those constituencies at the time I assumed office. The procedures used in the presidential search indicated that the college was being somewhat cautious in the important undertaking of interviewing candidates. The search committee, composed largely of trustees but including faculty, staff, and students, interviewed the seven semifinalists at a hotel near the airport. Some of the final interviews were held in the college-owned "presidential home" located fifteen miles from the college, with the outgoing president occasionally serving as an active participant.

The reactions of a group of the faculty and of the teachers union to my application for the presidency were interesting. Even though the faculty had representation on the formal presidential search committee, it was apparent that these groups undertook their own independent "review." During the search process, I learned from colleagues from my previous colleges of employment that some Stockton faculty were calling to inquire about my background. Questions were raised by those faculty about my publication record because a publishing date on one paper was very early in my career. (The article was published in 1953, when I was an undergraduate.) Furthermore, an arbitration decision regarding a personnel matter that had been under my purview was incorrectly interpreted. Anonymous negative comments about these and other issues were circulated at Stockton during the interview process. To the credit of these groups, when the truth about the matters under question was finally revealed, it was accepted. Nevertheless, such activities did not appear to be undertaken with respect to the other finalists, none of whom was a minority.

The students seemed to be the most delighted with my selection as president by the Board of Trustees. Despite a rumor laced with bias, that I went through college as an academically disadvantaged, "educational opportunity" student, the members of the student government and the student body were respectful in their interactions with me. Perhaps the fact that I had been an active and visible vice president for academic affairs at a northern New Jersey college, where I developed a reputation for being student-oriented, was helpful in my relations with students.

The administrative organization at Stockton was undergoing a controversial "changing of the guard" that was part of the subject of the legal dispute among the constituents. A brief period of respite was needed before this area could be assessed and the beginnings of an administrative team formed. Therefore, the administrators greeted my appointment as president with "cautious pessimism."

The response of the local community, as judged through the news media, was one of interest and curiosity — the novelty of a *female* president, because in 1983 there still were very few women college presidents across the nation. The fact that the new president also was African American gave rise to some comments about an "affirmative action" candidate. And so, in general, the community's attitude was "wait and see."

Two factors appeared to serve as important buffers for me. One element was the fact that, as a native of Atlantic City, which is seven miles from Stockton, I had gone through elementary and secondary schools in New Jersey. Many of my teachers, family, friends, and classmates still lived in the area. Also, my previous role as the vice president for academic affairs had been at Kean College, which is in northern New Jersey. In fact, my arrival at Kean was marked with a great deal of similar media interest, because in 1980 there also were very few women or minorities in the role of academic vice president at colleges where the majority of students and faculty were white. The same was true when I became the top academic officer at the SUNY at Brockport.

In the interviews during the presidential search process, the trustees raised several questions related to race, for example: "We have a very serious policy on affirmative action; it states that 50% of all hires must be with affirmative action and 25% must be minorities. What are your ideas on implementing our policy?" Another example: "Southern New Jersey often can be very conservative in its views about minorities. Are you prepared to live and work in this environment?"

I realized early on that all of my career in higher education as a faculty member and later as an administrator had been at colleges similar to Stockton — in other words, at predominantly white institutions. However, the other colleges were much larger in enrollment than Stockton. Apparently, the Stockton board of trustees had discussed among themselves the implications of selecting a female African-American president to administer a college composed predominantly of white faculty, students, and staff. And the largest percentage of each of these constituencies was male. Certainly, the trustees were aware of southern New Jersey's "conservative" reputation. Indeed, there have been several incidents that involved race or that had racial overtones during my tenure at Stockton. But in each instance, the trustees' support has been firm and unfaltering. As a body, they have never tolerated even a hint of racism toward the president. Nevertheless, my presidency has not been without incident.

Sometimes it is difficult to determine accurately whether the motivation of a specific group's action is racist, sexist, or some other "-ist." I certainly cannot hide the fact that I am an African-American woman. In 1989 a nationally known consultant was hired by the Stockton faculty assembly to make recommendations about faculty governance, staffing, and personnel guidelines. In his report, the consultant noted (under the rubric of racial tension) that "exceptions of significant sex discrimination, by way of contrast, do not appear to be nearly as wide-spread nor as deeply held" as racism. He also stated that this perception of racism was reinforced, in the eyes of the black faculty and staff, by what was seen as "vicious," "low, relentless" attacks on the president by some white colleagues.

Two specific examples of actions that "may have been influenced or affected by race" on my campus are as follows. The first situation occurred in early December 1985, when copies of a newsletter alternately titled "The Mad Hatter" and "Professor Trueheart" were circulated under the editorship of a former faculty union official. These newsletters had a "Dear Abby" format with alleged "letters" and "responses." The copy had a mocking tone in regard to me and often contained scurrilous, frequent reference to hats, which I often wear. A faculty group wrote three or so "volumes" of the newsletter (about 6 pages each) prior to designing a particularly chilling caricature, a large photograph of me with a bull's eye superimposed on the picture. On 13 December 1985, when people arrived on campus, these large, highly-visible, garish, bull's-eye pictures had been tacked up throughout the college's main buildings. The connotation of execution or assassination of the president was plain. In fact, the 1985 president of the faculty union wrote a letter to the entire Stockton community stating, "There is absolutely no place on this campus for the distribution of racist caricatures of the president of this institution. There is no cause, including the elimination of the tenure quotas, that justifies metastasizing the cancer of racism." Thereafter, no further copies of the newsletters, nor other hate-mongering caricatures, appeared in the public domain of the campus.

Another ugly situation occurred in April 1986. The office of the Atlantic County prosecutor initiated an investigation of alleged financial irregularities at Stockton State College, claiming to have in its possession some documentary evidence of wrongdoing. Three areas were investigated: 1) Stockton State College expenditures for official receptions, 2) a President's Fund checking account, and 3) travel reimbursements from two private boards on which I served as director. Fortunately, after a 24-week investigation including — according to the 23-page report — "aggressive interrogation" of the president, the prosecutor found no factual basis for prosecution of the matters cited and completely cleared me.

I should note that in mid-August 1986, a month before the completion of the prosecutor's investigation and before I or anyone could predict the outcome, I wrote a public letter to the entire college community stating that I had done nothing wrong and that it was my intention to provide a copy of the prosecutor's report to each member of the college whenever the investigation was ended. Therefore, on 19 September, the day the report was transmitted to the trustees, the trustees honored my request and distributed the prosecutor's report in its entirety to every member of the college community and to each constituency, internal and external to the college, including the chancellor, the foundation board, and other major organizations affiliated with the college. It was clear that I had engaged in no criminal conduct. Beyond that obvious conclusion, it was unequivocally shown that none of my actions, which were all closely reviewed, even hinted at any administrative or ethical improprieties.

Firmly believing that openness is the best defense against unwarranted attack, once the prosecutor's investigation was concluded, I immediately requested that the trustees launch their own investigation to determine whether I had committed any administrative improprieties or unethical activities. I also requested, before knowing the outcome, that the trustees' report be distributed to all members of the community. In my letter of request to the trustees I stated that, in fairness to me, this incident should not be "perceived merely as a roust and political skirmish." On 10 December 1986, the trustees completed their investigation and issued their report, which unequivocally cleared me of any and all wrongdoing with regard to administrative or ethical activities. I believed then, and do now, that had this investigation not been seriously and fully undertaken, the college collectively, and I personally, would have remained the victims of an insidious attack that sought to damage credibility and reputations.

Although the prosecutor's investigation was not overtly racially motivated, it appeared to create opportunities for race-related mischief. For example, the local newspaper wrote numerous articles about the prosecutor's investigation as front-page news with banner headlines, misleading and unattractive pictures, and degrading anecdotes. These lengthy articles appeared day after day, month after month, despite the fact that at no time was I charged with any criminal activity. The pictures were so unattractive that people wrote letters to the editor protesting this aspect of the investigation and demanding an apology from the newspaper for its obviously racist bias. Even after the prosecutor's report was transmitted and circulated, the local newspaper never once published an article drawing attention to the fact that I had been exonerated. Fortunately, the wide distribution of the prosecutor's report and the trustees' report throughout the college community, along with articles in the student newspaper, rapidly transmitted information to the larger community.

Many local groups, such as the NAACP, Jewish organizations, and the Anti-Defamation League, cited the news media's reporting of the investigation as examples of racism and prejudice. The trustees and I, however, did not want the college to become mired in a controversy over diversity. Thus we simply began to put the incident behind us and to move forward. As a result, Stockton College soon began a transformation process that developed the institution into a model of cooperation following these turbulent years of 1983 to 1986. A renewed sense of collegiality was established among the trustees, administration, students, and staff based on respect for each other's roles and on a mutual goal to work together in order for the college to succeed and thrive.

Somewhere along the process, Stockton's desire to build a premier liberal arts college won. The result was an amazing capacity of the college, once unified, to buck all of the current national trends. Several major accomplishments stand as measurable markers of this progress. The average total SAT of the entering students soared from 930 in 1983 to 1059 in fall 1995. The percentage of minority students doubled from 7% to 14% from 1983 to 1995. The percentage of minority faculty increased from 5% to 20%, and the percentage of female faculty increased from 23% to 38% in the same time.

By 1993 Stockton was ranked in the top 150 colleges and universities in North America. *U.S. News and World Report* ranked Stockton in the top 25% of Northern colleges and universities. The Carnegie Foundation classified Stockton in Category I for liberal arts colleges. On a regular basis Stockton has received recognition for excellence, including a full ten-year approval following external review by the Middle States Association accrediting body.

Once all of the college's constituents were able to communicate with one another without hostility, progress toward a unified purpose was swift and sure. It is necessary to convince faculty, staff, administration, and students that they have a stake in whatever problems exist at a college and that it will be to their common advantage to assist in devising ways to embrace diversity in order to find comprehensive solutions. If open and honest communication among the constituents can succeed in producing broad cooperation at a college or university, which is in essence a microcosm of society, it also can succeed in society at large. However, if the constituents leave a college carrying the same prejudices with which they entered, one wonders, ultimately, what college is all about.

Many discoveries and technological advances have emanated from our institutions of higher education. I am hopeful that the academy also can produce the solution to the human problems and provide a model of cooperation, of people living and learning in peace and harmony.

Carol C. Harter

TOUGH MIND, WARM HEART
by Carol C. Harter

Carol C. Harter is the president of the University of Nevada-Las Vegas, an office she assumed in July 1995, and the former president of the State University of New York at Geneseo. She earned a B.A. with Honors in English from Harpur College and M.A. and Ph.D. degrees in English and American literature from the State University of New York at Binghamton. She was a member of the English faculty at Ohio University while she served as university ombudsman, vice president and dean of students, and finally vice president for administration.

In 1989 Dr. Harter became president of SUNY at Geneseo, a college of 5,000 undergraduates and 350 graduate students. Her publications in the form of numerous articles, book chapters, and two books deal primarily with American literature, higher education, women, and leadership. Having received an honorary doctorate of humane letters from Ohio University, Dr. Harter has served as a consultant to that institution as well as to other colleges and corporations on such topics as strategic planning, program and performance evaluation, and women in management.

In the spring of 1961, at the tender age of 19, I decided to quit college, marry, have children, and probably never return to academic life even long enough to earn a bachelor's degree. My boyfriend (now husband of 35 years) also decided to quit school until we could afford to think of *his* returning at some indefinite point in the future. In 1961 a woman's return was not quite unthinkable, but it certainly was not a high priority.

Thus I present a study in contrasts. In 1989 I was inaugurated as the 11th — and first woman — president of the State University of New York at Geneseo. My husband, then dean of health and human services at Ohio University, would join me in New

York within the year when he became dean of professions at SUNY Brockport, a much shorter commute than we unhappily endured during my first year as a college president.

How, from such inauspicious beginnings, did we earn six degrees between us, raise two sons to productive adulthood (one is a teacher, the other an attorney), and embark on what must be judged by any measure a life full of incredibly attractive and fulfilling professional opportunities?

Some would say the answer lies in the genes. Others would argue nurture over nature and credit the land of unparalleled opportunity, opportunity made especially rich for women during the three decades I was developing my academic and administrative career. Mike and I often say that it was just a great deal of luck combined with good timing, plenty of hard work, and a shared tenacity that probably is genetic as well as sociological.

In any case, I attribute the real beginnings of my academic development to my early marriage, a supportive husband, and lack of money that "forced" me to visit the public library each week and return with six or seven books at a time for entertainment. (We did not even own a television set in those days.) Of course, my parents (and later, his) also influenced my career, albeit less directly.

Born in 1941 in Brooklyn of distinctly middle-class parents into a typical nuclear family of Irish/German/English backgrounds, I was the elder of two female Claney children. My father encouraged me to do just about anything, including play ball, accompanying him to Ebbets Field to see the Dodgers play twilight doubleheaders when I was a mere four years old. Although he encouraged me to excel, just as he would have an elder son, he also warned me not to become an "old maid," not to embark on a career that would take me away from traditional motherhood and wifely duties. Working in professional positions for 42 years with Mobil Oil, my father never did rise to the levels his intelligence and commitment to work would have suggested; but he believed somehow I might be capable of some vaguely imagined achievements, despite my womanhood.

My mother, always overtly dominated by my father, did not work and played the perfect nurturing role that was so typical of American women right after World War II. Although not possessed of a formal college education, my mother read voraciously, cared a great deal about the arts and my own aesthetic interests (I was both musically and artistically active), and encouraged me to do anything and everything to which I aspired. Indeed, I can honestly say that my mother — then and now — in some ways lived and lives vicariously through me, always supporting my aspirations unequivocally, while my father has never quite reconciled his sense of a woman's proper domesticity with his elder daughter's ambition, career accomplishments, and demands for total equality with all the men in her life. He is proud (to the point of embarrassment) of my accomplishments in the abstract, but finds it difficult to treat me in the flesh as anything other than his elder daughter, an ambivalence, one supposes, that characterizes most men born before World War I. My mother's relationship to me is happily less complex; we are straightforwardly devoted to each other, despite the marked differences in our lives.

Being raised on Long Island in the 1950s, surrounded by upwardly mobile middle-class peers, virtually all of whom aspired to the "best" colleges, I too had unrealistic expectations. I wanted to attend Duke or Cornell or Vassar and assumed I could, because I would be chosen the "outstanding senior" in my class for scholarship, leadership, and talent. However, my father made it clear that he could not afford to send me to any of these high-priced places and insisted that I avail myself of the opportunity to attend the "new college," then known as Harpur College, in Binghamton, a place created to join the highest academic experiences with low costs as part of the relatively new commitment to public higher education in New York. While I had the temerity to think Harpur beneath me, I went off to school — the first person on either side of the family who had the privilege of going away to a residential campus — with unfocused goals and a strong social agenda.

Although I was discouraged from attempting the chemistry major I was then considering (girls "didn't do" chemistry and math in

1959), I was strongly encouraged to study the humanities, particularly English, a field I had always thought too much fun for serious study. It all seemed too painless to mix some reasonably sophisticated reading with the freedoms of being a young woman finally out from under the oversight of a typically strict father of the 1950s.

And then I met Mike. He was a handsome and accomplished young man from upstate New York and the person who was to change my life and probably alter irrevocably what would have been a fairly predictable destiny. We dated in the fall of 1960, discovered sex, fell in love, and decided to marry and chuck formal schooling in 1961. From then on, life became very demanding, extremely difficult financially, and challenging in ways that apparently brought out some hidden reserves in each of us, some fundamental academic sensibilities, and the tenacity that would later lead to lives defined by shared commitments to demanding and rewarding careers in higher education.

We had a few months of living hand-to-mouth. Mike worked several menial jobs to earn our keep while I was pregnant, reading and painting to pass the time while I gestated. Then we decided that he, at least, needed to find a way to return to college, if only part-time. We were blessed with the new federal National Defense Education Act (NDEA), which offered us the few hundred dollars we needed to supplement the tuition Mike's generous, but financially strapped, parents provided. So Mike returned to Harpur and I, reading, in turn, all of Dostoyevsky, Virginia Woolf, Hemingway, Faulkner, and many others while I cared for our young son, started dreaming about my return to college as well.

The only way we could fulfill that dream was to borrow more money. Thus we applied for more NDEA loans and got them. We also decided to alternate class schedules in order to share the baby-sitting chores, a pattern that marked our lives and distinguished them from the married lives of many of our peers, whose sense of domestic roles was far more rigid than ours. Mike graduated in October of 1963, I in June of 1964, only a few months or a year later than our original class.

We were eager to begin the adult process of earning a decent living. Mike found a job teaching at an elementary Catholic school in Binghamton for a modest (even then) $4,000 a year. Much to my surprise, on my graduation I was offered the opportunity to continue in a newly formed master's in English program at what was then the emerging State University of New York at Binghamton. They were hungry for good graduate students to begin what became an almost meteoric rise to national recognition, which now characterizes Binghamton University. Where would they get these students? Why, among what Professor John V. Hagopian called the "housewives" of the undergraduate school, of course. And that is precisely what they got — including three of us who were simultaneously pregnant and filling the air in our Joyce seminar with the fecund spirit that was surely an appropriate accompaniment to the fertile monologues of Molly Bloom.

I continued in school, at first, not because I had ambitions beyond joining an English department in a local public school, but because I could remain at home with our son, nurture my second pregnancy, and earn a few dollars as a graduate assistant. Mike also was pursuing a master's degree part-time, so no untoward "competition" between husband and wife was then an issue.

As my graduate work advanced, however, I discovered things about myself that I had only dimly suspected: I cared deeply about literature and its formal study, I was a decent prose stylist and an eager scholar, and I could teach reasonably well — in fact, I loved college teaching.

Difficult personal times again intervened. I delivered a second healthy son but spent several months desperately ill with staph infections and multiple breast and gall bladder surgeries. As a result of slow recuperation, I was forced to suspend graduate study for almost a year.

Returning to Binghamton in the fall of 1966, I finished my master's degree and immediately was offered another assistantship, this time in the new Ph.D. program. (Cornell rejected me, telling my advisor I would get pregnant again and never finish Ph.D. work.) My mentor and advisor, Professor Hagopian, urged

125

me to consider an academic career; and that led to some of the first difficult discussions Mike and I ever had about priorities, gender roles, family values, and all the other conundrums that faced pioneering two-career couples. Although several members of our families and friends questioned the propriety of my earning a Ph.D. just as Mike was finishing his master's — and several more were stunned at the thought that I might be the one to secure a faculty position and Mike might, god forbid, actually follow *me* somewhere — we were able to strike a compromise that included my seeking a faculty position at a place that would offer Mike the opportunity to pursue a doctorate and that also offered an appropriate environment in which to raise two young children.

From among what turned out to be several very attractive offers at first-rate universities (in 1969, every English department wanted a woman), we chose Ohio University. I was delighted that they were truly interested in my teaching abilities and attitudes, not just in my scholarly potential. They were even generous enough to suggest that a 29-year-old "housewife" could actually teach graduate courses in contemporary American literature, even though I would be receiving my Ph.D. (with a "distinguished dissertation" on Faulkner) just three months before arriving in Athens, Ohio. The other attractive qualities about the place were its lovely, rural location (a wonderful place to raise sons) and its Ph.D. program in curriculum development, a field that interested Mike.

And so began what turned out to be a marvelous 19 years in Ohio. I was delighted with my professional friends and colleagues, and I had absolutely no sense that I would one day pursue any career other than that of full-time faculty member and scholar.

But the vicissitudes of life again intervened. Ohio University suffered a series of blows to its status and reputation that resulted in a loss of almost a third of its enrollments from 1970 to 1975. As a result, its budgetary support from the state plummeted. Unable to sustain the large new faculty and staff it had acquired in the 1960s, Ohio "retrenched" and laid off huge numbers of employees, including 90 nontenured faculty. I was one of those who received notice that I would not be rehired in 1975. I suffered what can only be called despair, convinced that, with two young children and a husband just emerging from a Ph.D. program, we would starve or be forced to take jobs outside academe.

With the help of several offices in the university, we tried to make an early affirmative action appeal, given the fact that I was one of only three women in a department of more than 50 members. Nothing worked. The senior faculty closed ranks and no criterion other than seniority was ultimately considered for those who would be retained. Hence, I got my first taste of administration through what I perceived as a fundamentally mindless approach to higher education "planning."

Without other recourse, I started looking for alternative employment and discovered one hopeful opportunity. Because Ohio University was in such turmoil and had entered a seemingly bottomless downward spiral, student and public criticism was leveled at the institution at every turn. So, despite the firing of hundreds of people, the position of ombudsman had been created with the hope that such a person could act as a safety valve for negative feelings and provide an outlet for grievances, particularly student grievances. I was nominated for the post by dozens of faculty colleagues who took up the cause and deluged the president with letters recommending me. However, I was convinced that the president (a lawyer, yet) would not choose me for the post, because he asked me how a woman with two small children and a working husband could handle this demanding job. But I also heard that his wife, also a lawyer, berated him for questioning me that way. I was delighted when the president asked me to become ombudsman.

I took on the task with zest and enthusiasm, working long hours and teaching a half-time load simultaneously. Although I did not know it consciously at the time, these two years prepared me in very special ways for administrative work, developing skills that remain invaluable to the art of leading an institution of higher education.

In the spring of 1975, the Ohio University trustees appointed Charles J. Ping, then provost at Central Michigan University, the

16th president of the university. Before he was to take office in July, Ping visited the troubled campus many times, noting how little planning took place there and how much internecine strife characterized the place. Ping had his work cut out for him and sought nontraditional sources of information in trying to understand an institution that felt itself under siege.

What so impressed me then — and continues to impress me now — was that Ping visited the ombudsman's office several times, disliking the idea that a university might *need* such an office, but simultaneously seeking my insights into just what areas of the institution seemed to be causing students and faculty the most problems. (Clearly, Ping believed that if the administration did its job correctly, no such ombudsman was required.)

Ping made the major structural and administrative changes that had become absolutely necessary. He instituted planning and made it come alive for the first time, connecting it directly to decision making and resource allocation, relationships that have since guided my own approach to campus leadership. He also reorganized the senior administration, recreating a dean of students position and elevating the academic vice presidency to provost. Students and others nominated me for dean of students, for which I felt absurdly unqualified, having never been responsible for a single administrative function.

On the other hand, having learned a good deal about administration from the ombudsman's point of view and having developed an almost reverential affection for the new president, I decided to throw my hat in the ring — but not before I talked seriously to my children (then 14 and 10) and not before I discussed with Mike the ways in which such a role, should I be appointed, would consume my life and theirs in ways we had never quite known before. Much to my surprise, they all supported me, though Mike was a bit concerned about what he knew would be my inability to capture all the moments one should capture as young boys become adolescents. In fact, our older son, always the rebellious one of the two, really surprised me when I described the opportunity to the boys. "Go for it, Mom," he said.

I have always been buoyed up by their support, and Mike's wonderful parenting often took over when I was increasingly involved in the responsibilities that define executive leadership.

I did indeed become the dean of students, a 35-year-old woman faculty member/ombudsman, inheriting massive enrollment management and operational problems, low staff morale and labor unrest, disaffected students, and a virtually bankrupt residence hall system. I was naive and idealistic enough to approach these formidable problems with a commitment to improve all of them as rapidly as possible and a totally unfounded belief in my own ability to accomplish these tasks. I thrived on the activity and on the challenges, working nights and weekends, learning new skills and gaining administrative knowledge, and becoming, for the first time in my career, a controversial figure who had to make difficult, sometimes unpopular decisions. I believe it was a role that women find particularly painful to assume. But I persevered. In the summer of 1977, I attended the Institute for Educational Management (IEM) program at Harvard because Charlie Ping invested in and provided me with the professional development experience necessary for any ingenue to succeed, perhaps particularly for a woman, the first woman to be placed in such a senior role in the long history of Ohio University.

I was promoted to vice president and dean of students in 1977, a year also characterized by difficult marital problems, painful teenage growth problems, and general domestic tension and conflict. Fortunately, our long marriage and strong affection for each other, as well as mutual tenacity and a combined refusal to succumb to difficult times, saw us through these years when Mike finished his doctorate and Sean, our younger son, graduated from high school and began college. He would graduate *summa cum laude* in three years and then earn a law degree.

Although I started exploring some external career opportunities, President Ping restructured senior administration once again and offered me an entirely new role as vice president for administration, which gave me a chance to learn a whole new area of university life as well as to acquire additional management skills

129

in operations that women traditionally do not manage. These were heady experiences for a woman, the only woman in this role in any of Ohio's major public institutions. I also tried to mentor and promote other women and minorities who heretofore had not had opportunities in the "hard" management arenas that finance and administration traditionally represent on our campuses.

Teaching and scholarly work, however, also remained important to me, even during these challenging times of administrative restructuring. I team-taught periodically and began a series of dialogues with Jim Thompson about American novelists that would later translate into two co-authored books.

But even the teaching and research did not forestall my inevitable self-discovery that administrative work needed to be grounded in academic matters for me to be fully satisfied. I realized that my choices were, ironically, either to return to full-time teaching or to seek a presidency where, ideally, I would be able to concern myself, at least to some extent, with the heart of higher education: its academic programs and its students.

Because Mike had by this time become dean of health and human services at Ohio and was enjoying his role enormously, the decision to seek a presidency was extremely difficult for me and controversial between us. But there was no doubt that I was ready. SUNY Geneseo's presidency was especially compelling, though it was not the first nomination I accepted.

Against everyone's advice, I pursued the opportunity, soon becoming a finalist. Neither of my sons thought I would take the job, and my father was utterly dumbfounded when I did, shocked at the thought that his daughter would consider leaving her husband — even temporarily — to fulfill her crass ambitions. To put it mildly, no one, including Charlie Ping, who thought SUNY entirely too bureaucratic for me, supported my decision. Even those who thought I should be a president somewhere were skeptical. So I made the choice by myself and cried for days once I had accepted. I recognized that this was a lonely decision I was making but was going to be the right one after all. And the college has been wonderful, the presidency enormously rewarding. After a rocky, lonely first year, Mike made the very difficult, indeed self-sacrificing decision to leave his most gratifying deanship at Ohio for an interesting, but less prestigious, lateral position in New York.

What I find most satisfying in my presidency are the people — students, faculty, and staff — and Geneseo's focus on being the premier public undergraduate institution in New York. Recently honored by the Rochester Women's Network as "Woman of the Year," I take great personal satisfaction in being a role model for the many outstanding female students and for hiring and promoting many more women faculty and staff than any of my predecessors had.

I believe there are some leadership characteristics that can be emulated by anyone trying to provide truly inspired direction and life to a college or university. Ten such traits are the following:

- *Perceiving and articulating shared goals:* By listening to people from across disciplines, constituencies, and campus/community lines, one should be able to discern the essence and possible future directions of a college or university.

- *Developing a future orientation:* Leaders can never rest on their laurels; leaders know that every organization is in constant flux and must change continuously to improve and to maintain high quality.

- *Establishing a leadership tone and presence:* Women need to gain confidence and learn they can self-consciously establish an effective public presence, a leadership tone, just as men do naturally.

- *Sublimating the ego:* The best leaders — men or women — sublimate even exquisitely sensitive egos and the need for personal praise and acceptance by thinking in terms of the well-being of the institution they serve, recognizing that individual success is meaningless unless the institution is successful.

- *Indulging a people-orientation:* Women should feel comfortable exercising this natural orientation; in higher education, all goals and all work should reflect a commitment to the development of people.

- *Embodying and encouraging teamwork:* Women need to understand the dynamics and ground rules of teamwork to which men come already, sometimes unconsciously, prepared.
- *Becoming politically sensitive while retaining integrity:* The two are not mutually exclusive, though women tend to think "politics" is a dirty word.
- *Getting fit and staying healthy:* While we cannot create healthy bodies merely by imposing some magic formula, much good health is self-willed and represents a determination not to succumb to petty physical annoyances; taking care of oneself is an obligation of leaders.
- *Enjoying ourselves:* Women need to take themselves a little less seriously, indulging a sense of humor and creating a thicker skin.
- *Doing the ordinary extraordinarily well:* There are small acts — treating subordinates extremely well — that humanize us in ways that create an environment of shared goals and values.

What finally makes the most effective leaders in today's world? When I think of the most effective people over the long haul, I think of the most human: those who occasionally display their vulnerability, who demonstrate their deep caring for friends and family and integrate those feelings and relationships into public life, who occasionally choose relationships over ambition, privacy over public displays, nurturing over ordering.

On the personal level, I am immensely enriched by the extraordinary strength of our marriage, by the small, but lovely house we have bought on Lake Ontario where our private lives are private, and by the love we share with our children. We are grateful, and occasionally amazed, at how blessed we are.

Postscript

I accepted the presidency of the University of Nevada-Las Vegas in February 1995 and began that work on 1 July 1995. Mike and

I again are experiencing a commuter marriage that I hope can be ended within a year or less, assuming he finds a role that he wishes to pursue in the West. Thus the saga of the two-career couple continues.

Bette E. Landman

NURTURING CHANCE: AN ACCIDENTAL LIFE
by Bette E. Landman

Bette E. Landman is the president of Beaver College in Glenside, Pennsylvania. She graduated summa cum laude *from Bowling Green State University with a B.S. in elementary education before receiving M.A. and Ph.D. degrees in anthropology with honors from Ohio State University. After teaching fifth-grade in Ohio and anthropology at Springfield College, Temple University, and Beaver College, Dr. Landman assumed the administrative positions of dean of the college, vice president for academic affairs, and acting president of Beaver College before becoming president.*

Bette Landman has received fellowships from the National Science Foundation and the Wenner-Gren Foundation for Anthropological Research, doing research in the Caribbean Sea. Dr. Landman's professional activities include participation in the Harvard Institute for Educational Management, chair of the board of directors of the Association of American Colleges, president of the board of directors of the Commission for Independent Colleges and Universities and of the Association of Presbyterian Colleges and Universities, and board member of the American Council on Education and the Pennsylvania Association of Colleges and Universities.

I recall Margaret Mead once telling the students of Beaver College that there is a cultural chasm between those born before World War II and those brought into the world after that time. I feel the weight of that statement as I compose this document, wondering if my story and my experiences will have any meaning for the young women who will lead higher education in the next century.

I was born the middle child in a small Ohio town in 1937, but my father quickly took his wife and three children to San Francisco. I think that he was eager to sever the ties to his hometown and spread his wings in a cosmopolitan setting. A rare photograph from that period shows him on the beach in knit swim trunks looking very much like a thin, confident Cesar Romero (a suave, then-popular film star). The marriage, however, was not working. My mother was scarcely ever home, and my father became essentially the parent of influence for the first ten years of my life — for the years in California and later for the four years back in Ohio, when we were living with my great aunts who had raised my father after his mother had died.

I start my story here, for I believe that the basic values and personality traits that have shaped my life, both personally and professionally, stem from these early years. I can see the trauma caused by an often-absent mother, by a San Francisco of wartime blackouts, and later by life with great aunts dying of cancer. Such things left both permanent scars and special strengths of character in my siblings. I must assume a similar influence on me. Whether these traits are a help or a hindrance in my professional life, I leave to the reader to determine.

What were the early learnings? First and foremost, I was blessed with a father who saw parenting as his most rewarding and important role. He self-consciously determined that children should be treated honestly if they were to become honest (and honesty was the value he deemed most important), that they should not be scolded or spanked, and that performance standards should be internally, not externally, imposed. He loved learning and wanted his children to love books and intellectual challenge. He read voraciously, if not widely. I remember many evenings when we children tried to stump my father with questions about history. He nearly always won.

In many ways, I bought into these values. I, too, have treasured honesty as the most important value. I have sometimes modified it by my great aunt's dictum, "If you can't say something nice, don't say anything at all," but I truly believe that openness and truth ultimately win the day in any assignment or relationship. Like my father, reading is still my preferred window on the world. At the same time, I believe that I would have profited by more discipline and task orientation early in my life. I often find it difficult to begin a project that I find daunting or unexciting; but once the job is tackled, I tend to be relentless until it is done. This energy has served me well as an administrator, just as the procrastination has served me ill.

Second, I suspect that the unpredictability of my early life led me to find reward in making few demands and in being a compliant child. I clearly wanted praise and acceptance but was uncomfortable in the spotlight. I still find these two needs in conflict.

Third, I learned to be self-reliant. My father remarried when I was ten, but within a year and a half he was gravely injured. Family savings went to hospital bills. My father was bedridden for more than a year and thereafter his choice of jobs was severely limited. Even with my stepmother working, discretionary money was in short supply. I started babysitting at age ten and so was able to buy most of my own clothes and school supplies; by 16 I combined babysitting with work at a local department store. I remember feeling pained but not devastated when my siblings and I could not have the same things that friends seemed to have. It made all three of us more creative. While friends received purchased doll clothes, I made mine. My sister was able to go into the best dress shop and study the clothes, which she then duplicated on our home sewing machine. Today I still see unrequited wishes as problems to be solved, not obstacles to action. On the other hand, it was not until I was a college administrator that I had the good fortune to have a dean of students help me learn that to receive is as generous an act as to give; and that it is all right to hire services done, even if you are capable of doing the work yourself.

I wish I could say that these early life experiences gave me the drive to set and pursue clearly perceived career and personal goals. They did not. Instead, I was and still am a person to whom opportunities have happened, not one who created them. And yet, perhaps, my willingness to take advantage of such chances when they have occurred may somehow be a product of that same past.

As I reflect on my career, I see most strongly the influence and kindness of teachers, mentors, and friends. I had not dreamed of going to college until two high school teachers approached my parents with an offer to recommend me for a full scholarship to a state university to study elementary education. With no funds to spare, I completed undergraduate study in two years and two summers and began to teach fifth grade. The opportunity for graduate study in anthropology came suddenly and unexpectedly, the result of a truly chance encounter during a friend's visit to Ohio State University.

The years at OSU, though unusual in certain ways, were, I see now, extensions of the me that had been forming. I studied physical anthropology at the master's level not by choice but by following the random assignment of an advisor, despite the fact that I had not one prerequisite for the graduate-level anatomy, embryology, and medical school coursework that the program entailed. As an undergraduate, I never even had a laboratory course. I also allowed that advisor to co-opt me into grading all of his and another professor's classroom papers, even though my OSU scholarships specifically excluded me from acting as a teaching assistant.

In hindsight, this exploitation had mixed outcomes. The experience forced me to learn each subject in sufficient depth to ensure that my fellow students were being treated fairly. At the same time, two of my major professors never read any of my examinations or papers, including my master's thesis. I was (and continue to be) an insecure writer. My high school had not been demanding, and now my graduate work was not helping me to obtain greater facility in clear and cogent expression. Typically, I did not complain or ask for a different advisor. In fact, I continued to work with this professor until I had completed all my coursework and fieldwork for the doctorate. Indeed, *he* terminated the role as advisor after I awkwardly failed to respond to his indirect request for an intimate relationship. By then, I was already teaching at a small college in Massachusetts; and though my new advisor was intelligent, diligent, and supportive, it took me six years to finish the writing of my dissertation. In fact, I might never have finished the doctorate had it not been for her persistence. She had been the professor I had come most to admire and respect, and her assurances that there was a quality product in what I was doing helped to get me back on track.

I taught anthropology for 12 years, three as the only anthropologist at a small college, then four at a university where I erroneously thought I would be happier immersed in the discipline, and five at a small college where I was again the only anthropologist.

My fieldwork, in 1964-65, was on a small island in the Caribbean. I was studying how families organized themselves when one-third of the male population emigrated, leaving ten adult women for every six adult men. Fieldwork was a time to test my mettle. Was I the adaptable person I thought myself to be? Was I truly self-reliant? The island had no running water and no electricity, but I clearly was not in the wilds of some country as the first outsider to penetrate a primitive culture. Still, there were lonely problem-solving challenges that marked my early weeks and rare times when I wondered whether I was cut out for this kind of experience. I rejoiced when things went well, sometimes even better that I had a right to expect, but worried that I might not be doing the very best work that could be done.

This duality — joy and worry — has characterized each new academic career I have pursued. I recall feeling somewhat as though I were again in a foreign culture when in 1976 I accepted the challenge to become academic dean at Beaver College. I had been teaching there for five years as an assistant professor just coming up for tenure when the dean of one year announced that he would be departing in three weeks. The president met with that dean's search committee and announced that he would find it acceptable to have an interim dean from the faculty. He suggested two names; mine was one. When I was told, I assumed that the teller was kidding me — no one could possibly think of me in this capacity, surely neither the president nor the faculty. When I was assured that the offer was indeed real, I was both frightened and disoriented. Here again I was about to plunge into something for which I felt ill-prepared.

Ultimately, I accepted the challenge of the deanship; and somewhat to my surprise, I found the position stimulating. In part, this was because of the incredible tolerance and generosity of the faculty and staff as I stumbled up the learning curve. Despite my having come out of the faculty, not one individual tried to use friendship or our collegial relationship for personal gain. Collectively, the faculty understood the boundaries of our restructured roles and found avenues to maintain our personal ties in new, uncompromising ways. An unanticipated bonus to the new position was the new colleagues I was meeting at regional and national conventions of academic deans and vice presidents. Also, I greatly enjoyed the chance to see the college and higher education as whole systems. I liked to interact with colleagues across disciplinary boundaries, and I found taking part in institution-wide committees rewarding. As dean, I missed the classroom; but I was finding the new, larger arena equally engaging.

What I did not anticipate was the degree to which a dean's time and energy were controlled by the position. As a diligent teacher and campus participant, I suspect I was putting in about 70 hours per week, but those hours usually were reasonably flexible. As dean, the time was equally demanding, but the hours were largely beyond my control. Increasingly, my personal life became further constrained as I was expected to spend "social" time with people designated by the college — alumni, community organizations, and others. Most unexpected and revealing, however, was the view that I had into the "backstages" of faculty lives. In counseling and evaluating faculty, I came to see discrepancies between projected personae and real accomplishment, discrepancies that went both ways. Most important, I learned that those whose assessments of themselves are at odds with reality are those who present the most taxing and emotionally draining of the personnel issues that challenge us.

In a strange way, the president who had suggested me for the dean's role was both a mentor and a model from whom I learned how and how *not* to lead. A kind and caring man, he set a cooperative tone for the college that in many ways still characterizes the institution. He was at the helm during the salad days of the 1960s and then during the 1970s when the college plunged into financial uncertainty. His indecisive leadership style empowered faculty and others to take initiative, but it equally frustrated these groups as they saw important presidential roles in fundraising and institutional integration being neglected. Announcing their frustration, some of the most supportive members of the board of trustees resigned, leaving a group behind that did not ask about or know the true condition of the college. My sense is that the president retreated into kindness and gentleness, protected against collective confrontation by dealing one-on-one with trustees, faculty, and senior staff.

From the situation at Beaver and the expanding roles I was playing in regional and national associations, I soon concluded that an effective leader needed a team of advisors diverse in opinion and willing to challenge a president when their positions differed. Similarly, a healthy college must have board members who are fully informed about the strengths and weaknesses of the college and willing to ask the hard questions. I also learned that senior staff, including deans, must set limits on their roles as message-carriers from the president, thereby forcing the president to speak with his own voice in critical areas. A president does not lose by being perceived as an individual who can make hard decisions and still be caring. In the final analysis, being respected may be more important than being beloved.

These lessons soon were to be tested, when the president of 23 years became terminally ill in 1982. On the last day of the first real vacation I had taken since I became dean, I was informed that a message already had gone to the campus that I was the acting president. I was never permitted to speak to the president to find out what was pending and what needed urgent attention. The "official" line after mid-September was that he would be back in two weeks, and so there was no need for conversation. Those "two weeks" were constantly extended until he died in January.

Not surprisingly, my acting presidency was filled with both frustration and reward. Because the president was always "two weeks away from returning to work," the board neither initiated a reduction in my duties as dean nor proffered a change in salary, despite my carrying the dual position for 13 months. (The treasurer finally reminded the trustees that some adjustment in compensation was warranted.) However, the faculty and staff fully realized the extra burden and offered to take on as many of the duties of the dean as they could knowledgeably fulfill. This was one of the most affecting and affirming experiences I could have had during this hectic time.

But on the whole, I was sufficiently disenchanted with my experience as acting president to refuse an offer from the board to be nominated for the vacancy. I felt my greater service would be to help the trustees understand the reality of the college's strengths and weaknesses and to position the college for the selection of an appropriate new leader. I also knew that the internal community was looking for a paragon who, with consummate skill, would correct all the perceived ills of the institution. No one from inside the college was likely to be afforded the breathing space that a stranger would be given.

I also realized that it was probably time for me to move on. I had served for nine years as dean and academic vice president. My wonderfully supportive mentoring group in the Office of Women of the American Council of Education in Washington had been urging me for several years to begin thinking about a presidency elsewhere. I informed the new president at Beaver that I was on the market and began to follow up on several nominations.

However, leadership at the college was again faltering. Perhaps no president could have fulfilled the long-deferred expectations of the Beaver community. I decided to stay for one more year, only to find myself again as acting president. This time, interviews at other institutions, enhanced understanding of the duties of a president in a normal setting, and greater distance from my role under the previous president, persuaded me — albeit reluctantly — to acquiesce to the board's request to stand for nomination as president. The search process was stormy and the final choice was not one on which all internal parties agreed. But again the community openly shared its feelings and then vowed to get on with support of me as the board's choice.

I was inaugurated as president of Beaver College in 1985, and so I have now been in this position for slightly more than a decade. Many of my earlier discoveries and understandings have served me well. I have built a diverse and talented team that I feel is candid with me and with each other. Building such a team did not come easily. Long-term employees — good people whose skills and orientations were not consonant with the college as it needed to become — had to be let go. Similarly, the board of trustees had to be restructured. I was fortunate in having a board chair who took on the task of rewriting the bylaws and took seriously the need to transform the board from an honorary, self-perpetuating body into a working, knowledgeable group of advisors. Financially, some hard, short-term decisions caused great consternation; but I had long since learned that angry accusations and even a faculty work slowdown were not necessarily personal attacks — learning made easier by the ability of the faculty themselves not to carry anger beyond the bounds of a meeting or an act.

The presidency also honed my skill for seeing the institution in its entirety. Survival meant that day-by-day and year-by-year the institution had to position itself for greater financial security and clarity of mission. We had to define who we were and make our goals clear. I, and we, were not as skilled planners in those early days as I would have wished. Goals were sometimes vague and outcomes were not always expressed in measurable terms. As we roll up the newest five-year plan, I feel more secure about our abilities to plan well. The president's role in guiding the institution is one of the real joys of the position. I know that I cannot unilaterally impose a vision on the college, but setting the stage and general direction and nurturing its emergence are truly rewarding.

My belief that honesty is one key to good administration is unshaken. In the classroom and in the office, I have learned that you do not lose the respect of others when you honestly admit what you do not know. You also can be honest in revealing to others that certain information must be kept confidential. Another critical component of honesty is being able to accept blame when you have not performed well, have misjudged, or have been remiss.

Honesty operates hand-in-hand with being fair. Those making requests will accept a refusal if they feel confident that you do not reward others on the basis of personal ties or special pleadings. In real life, of course, these decisions are not clear cut. But for me, honesty and fairness form a defining characteristic that I think of as integrity. It is a kind of invisible line that, if crossed, would force me to lose touch with my true self.

I have learned two other lessons, but at times they seem in opposition. The first is to trust my instincts. The second is to be a good listener. There is some magical, not always knowable, boundary demarcating these two. When should one take the sage advice of others and when should one listen to that vague inner voice warning that reason must give way to right?

In some ways, the position of president echoes and heightens skills and understandings gleaned from a deanship. Certainly the demands on personal time become greater, and more and more of one's life is dictated by the needs of the college. The rich opportunities for learning expand, now covering such non-deanly topics as building bonds, facilities management, and sewer systems. But in other ways the dean's position does not prepare one for a presidency. As dean, I underestimated the importance of the trustees. Building a strong and involved board is one of the most important tasks for a president of an independent college.

The weight of guiding the college also takes on a special immediacy in the presidency. Most higher education institutions today are fragile. Finding that right balance between prudence and risk may be key to a college's future ability to thrive. Despite some pleas to the contrary, today's presidents truly do have the chance to lead. What frightens me is whether we — and I — will have the resources and the will to address the pressing needs for access and equity.

New experiences and new positions have a way of forcing us to probe our inner selves and, hopefully and almost invariably, to find bits of our being that would have lain dormant had we not taken on the new challenge. But we also are carriers of our own past baggage. At the beginning of this essay, I noted that I chose

144

to start my story with my early childhood because I felt that much that I learned then was still shaping my life. Some of those learnings, I believe, have served me well in the various roles I have assumed; others are areas with which I am still struggling. I still crave recognition from others but find myself embarrassed when it is given. My desire to speak up in public forums on issues about which I feel passionate has grown, and yet I have never quelled the stage fright that each presentation or leadership position occasions. I think of myself as one who has learned to "roll with the punches," but I regret that I have never set myself on a more purposive life career path. I still envy those who tackle a task immediately after it is assigned and those who can write a polished document on the first draft. Despite years of work, my writing is still pedestrian and needs the hand of a good editor.

I'm still trying to learn how and when to delegate and how to fully empower others. I am not always good at judging what is responsible oversight, what is imposition (taking unfair advantage of others' goodwill), and what is empowerment. Yet I constantly am surprised by the tolerance of those with whom I deal. They have overlooked my shortcomings and ignored my oversights. I still feel that this generosity often is unwarranted, and maybe someday the real, less able me, will be exposed.

Perhaps in this personal list of felt deficiencies, the reader will get some further sense of what tasks and abilities are valuable components of an effective presidency. Perhaps, too, this is a meaningful way of bringing this story full circle. In our own special ways, we are the product of our life's varying experiences. For me, the fulfilled life is one in which we constantly push at the envelope of our being, setting ourselves new challenges and balancing what we know we can do with what we have yet to discover we might be able to do.

Elizabeth Llewellyn-Smith

FROM WHITEHALL TO CHERWELL
by Elizabeth Llewellyn-Smith

Elizabeth Llewellyn-Smith is principal of St. Hilda's College, Oxford University. She attended Christ's Hospital (a private girls' boarding school) before earning First Class B.A. and M.A. degrees in history from Girton College, Cambridge University. One of her brothers was chairman of physics at Oxford University and received the Maxwell Prize and Medal from the Institute of Physics; another brother is the British ambassador to Poland.

After university, Ms. Llewellyn-Smith joined the Civil Service and held various appointments in the Board of Trade, the Department of Trade and Industry, the Cabinet Office, and the Department of Prices and Consumer Protection. In 1977 she became the first woman to attend the Royal College of Defence Studies. After serving as deputy director general of fair trading, chairman of the merger panel in the Office of Fair Trading, deputy secretary of the Department of Trade and Industry, and a director of the European Investment Bank, Ms. Llewellyn-Smith was appointed principal of St. Hilda's.

My background is conventional English middle class, with the pluses and minuses that description entails. My father was a schoolmaster, his professional career interrupted by service in the Royal Air Force during the Second World War. My mother had no career of her own after her marriage in 1933. That was common form at the time and hardly surprising for someone who eventually had five young children in tow. My twin sister and I were born in 1934 and the next brother within 18 months.

On both sides, the family took higher education for granted. My mother was one of five, all educated at Oxford or Cambridge. My father was one of six, of whom five were educated at Oxford and one at London University. All ended up with conventional middle-class jobs in the professions or public service.

As children, we were not well off. We lived in a cottage in a remote village in Yorkshire while my father was in the Air Force. Neither money nor food was plentiful in the days of wartime rationing. We attended a village elementary school at a period when this was unusual for professional families. However, our cottage was full of books, and it was simply taken for granted that my sister, my brothers, and I would progress through school to university.

By a stroke of good fortune, my twin sister and I were nominated at the age of 12 for places at Christ's Hospital, the famous bluecoat charity school. While conditions there were Spartan, the school was academically first rate. In those days there were two separate Christ's Hospital schools, one for boys and one for girls. They have since merged. My experience of a small, single-sex, girls' boarding school and of an all-women's college at Cambridge left me with no hang-ups about single-sex education.

I went to Girton College, Cambridge, on a scholarship to read history and graduated with a First Class degree in 1956. My sister and brothers were all undergraduates at Oxford.

Graduate employment was not a problem in the 1950s. Opting for the familiar course of the Civil Service Selection Board, I took up a post as an assistant principal in the Board of Trade in September 1956, arriving in time to have a hand in the residual activities of postwar rationing and physical controls. For young civil servants in the 1950s and 1960s, promotion was slow and the emphasis was on breadth of experience. In a remote department dealing with tourism, I was at one moment honing the arguments for retiming the August Bank Holiday, at another drafting a speech for celebration of the 900th anniversary of the Battle of Hastings.

In more senior posts, two themes came to predominate — the handling of parliamentary legislation and the promotion of competition. I had a hand in the bills that became the Resale Prices Act, the Monopolies and Mergers Act, the Fair Trading Act, and the European Communities Act, which "took Britain into Europe." That was a stroke of luck, indeed. I was in the right place at the right time, having been posted to the Cabinet Office for a totally different purpose — the wash-up on the fiasco of the Rolls Royce RB 211 engine — when the Cabinet Office for the first time found itself charged with the executive responsibility for handling that major piece of legislation — and looked around for someone to run the bill team. Before departing that post, I earned a word of praise from Secretary of the Cabinet Sir Burke Trend for leaving the papers well-prepared for the future archivist or constitutional historian.

A year's semi-sabbatical in 1977 was spent at the Royal College of Defence Studies, the first woman to attend that college. It was a marvelous year, providing opportunities for visits to the British Army of the Rhine and to China, Japan, Korea, and Hong Kong in the closing days of the Cold War and the aftermath of the "smashing of the Gang of Four." At the very least, it set up a network of good friends in all three services.

In 1978, I returned to the Department on Promotion to take charge of the Companies Division. I was promoted again in 1982 to become a deputy to the director general of Fair Trading. In the Office of Fair Trading my time as chair of the Merger Panel coincided with the thrills and spills of the 1980s mergers book and some of the *causes célèbre* of that era (House of Fraser, Guinness, and so on).

My final civil service appointment involved a return to the Department of Trade and Industry where (in contrast to earlier posts in the *laissez-faire* trade side of the department) I was in charge of so-called regional policy and the subvention of investment in assisted areas.

I was invited in 1989 to apply for the position of principal of St. Hilda's College and took up that post in August 1990. The heads of Oxford colleges are elected by the Fellows. They have no independent executive authority. And it is not done to inquire about the competition or why a particular person was elected. I can only deduce that my administrative experience was held to be helpful to the college. Perhaps the competition was not that strong. St. Hilda's College is one of Oxford's poorer colleges and its single-sex status will not be everyone's cup of tea. The salary of a principal, linked to the Oxford professional salary, would be regarded as risible in most professions and is a living wage only for someone with a pension from earlier employment or other means.

Since I became principal, the single-sex constitution of my college has become more distinctive. St. Hilda's College is now the only Oxford college that does not admit men. We intend, if we can, to remain a women's college in order to offer a single-sex option to potential students and a step on the tenure track to women scholars.

There is no job description for the head of an Oxford college. Our statutes simply require that the woman concerned "shall be elected by the members of the governing body who are entitled to vote" and "shall be the person who in their judgment is most fitted for the headship of the college as a place of religion, learning, and education." No specific qualifications are prescribed. Colleges sometimes elect academics from among their own membership, sometimes outsiders with contacts or qualities that they think may be helpful. Since all colleges are actively fundraising, increasing weight today is placed on the ability to motivate alumnae and tap corporate or charitable sources of finance.

The position is very much what the holder makes it and, to be frank, carries a good deal less responsibility and freedom of action than many incumbents will have found elsewhere. At the same time it is immensely rewarding and enjoyable, with the opportunity to know and influence new generations of young people and to meet the range of crazy, brilliant, and infuriating people who make up the collegiate university of Oxford.

Mary Patterson McPherson

TWO AFTERNOONS
ON THE JOB
by Mary Patterson McPherson

Mary Patterson McPherson is president of Bryn Mawr College. After attending Agnes Irwin School, a girls' school where her mother was a teacher, Mary P. McPherson received an A.B. degree with honors from Smith College, an M.A. from the University of Delaware, and a Ph.D. in philosophy from Bryn Mawr College. She taught philosophy at the latter two institutions before ascending the administrative ranks at Bryn Mawr, from assistant and associate dean of the college, to dean, acting president, and finally president in 1978.

Dr. McPherson's research interests include the philosophy of F.H. Bradley and 19th century British idealism. The recipient of honorary degrees from nine institutions (including the University of Pennsylvania, Princeton University, Swarthmore College, Haverford College, and Smith College), Dr. McPherson is a present or past director or board member of the American Council on Education, the Carnegie Foundation for the Advancement of Teaching, the Carnegie Corporation of New York, the Spencer Foundation, the Josiah Macy Foundation, the Brookings Institution, Bell Telephone Company of Pennsylvania, Phillips Exeter Academy, Wilson College, and Amherst College, among others.

I am a walker for sport and recreation, and I have to admit from the outset that I take a somewhat different view of the "career path" than most people do. The path itself, the visibly trodden way, is less interesting to me than the scenery along the way. Perhaps this is because the steps toward my current position have been rather ordinary ones. I went to elementary school, high school, and college; I entered graduate school, took a Ph.D., and taught; I accepted the offer of an assistant deanship where I was studying and teaching and went on to serve as associate dean, as dean of the college, as acting president, and finally as president — the straightest of ladders, in one sense, a well-worn path.

At the same time, I have found the people and the issues around me engrossing and the challenges exhilarating at every step of the way. Scenery is, of course, far too light and superficial a term for the rich environment of human transformation and institutional dynamics that constitute education in the United States today. Education always has seemed to me to be worth everything, worth giving the best of one's energies, worth devoting oneself to wholly.

The two women who gave me the gifts of their experience, example, and encouragement did so not by relating to me their life stories but by allowing me to live and work for some years in their presence. My mother was a teacher in the girls' school that I attended, and I grew up breathing in, like fresh air, her zest for her work and her belief in its value. Later, when I went to Bryn Mawr as a doctoral student, I had the privilege of beginning my administrative career under the auspices of the college's extraordinary fourth president, Katharine McBride, who eventually became a friend. She, too, simply carried on her work in my presence so that I felt her devotion and wisdom in action.

And so it seems to me that the most vivid way of conveying the essence of my own experience is by inviting the reader to accompany me for two afternoons that stand out in my memory as significant occasions for women on their own paths to leadership. The first of these afternoons was in January 1992, when I had been asked to deliver a keynote speech to a conference at Bryn Mawr College on "Women in Leadership." That was my topic. Most members of the audience were undergraduate women students from area colleges, a group that will very soon take their places in leadership roles in all areas of our society. In part, what I said to them is this:

It is sometimes a good idea to begin considering a complex topic like leadership by stating the obvious, or at least what passes for the obvious at some time and place. This gives us a momentary clarity from which to start as we plunge into the often elusive and difficult subject. And what seems obvious about leadership in our time is that it is intimately bound up with the process of social change. It is historically clear that certain individuals stand in a special relation to the currents of movement and change in their culture.

But right away an element of uncertainty and controversy enters the matter, for historians are by no means in agreement about what that special role of that leading individual is. Is the leader the cause of the change, the originator of the trend, the active force pressing the sluggish elements of society forward? Or is the leader an effect of the change, an expression and peculiarly apt embodiment of larger currents which shape the personality like malleable clay and which call forth in certain individuals what is needed and formed by the times? Of course, this is not an either/or issue. Every one of us is to some degree both a product and a producer of the culture in which we live. We say yes to some things and no to others, and we are partly conditioned by our experiences and public world and partly free agents to consent or protest. We both shape and are shaped by the circumstances of our lives.

But just because these views are both true does not necessarily mean that they are equally true. I believe that it makes a very great difference how you balance the two sides, where the weight of your emphasis and the power of your conviction falls. A French historian, Fernand Braudel, once wrote, "Men are unable to make history. They can only watch it happen, like a television program." This spectator's view of history can have profound effects on people's actions as citizens, leading them to detachment and apathy, to a view of history as someone else's business, someone else's story, even as nightly entertainment.

Other historians believe that people can make history in certain circumstances and certain ways. They believe that individuals do indeed make a difference, that in fact history is an aggregate of individuals making differences. A leader is someone who makes a bigger difference than others; but every person, however humble, merely by acting or not acting, makes a difference of some kind, makes errors of defect, as the mathematicians say, or errors of excess that, however insignificant they may seem at the moment, can have surprisingly large cumulative final effects. In this view, no one is free of the responsibility for making the history of the times.

Thus when you consider a leadership role for yourself or someone else, you are contemplating a very complex and unstable relation of one individual to the greater social body — be it a campus community, a neighborhood, a city, a region, a generation, a nation. All of our deepest questions and needs are writ large in the leader, who dramatizes for everyone the shifting and elusive relation of the one to the many, the individual to the masses; the relation of the past to the future; and the critical issues of weakness and power.

All the spheres of leadership overlap — this is a vital point for you to understand. The neighborhood makes a difference to the city; the campus makes a difference to the generation and the culture. No small group exists in isolation from the larger groups of which it is a part or from which it tries to distinguish itself. You may begin by leading a classroom of children or a family, a social club or an athletic team, a committee or a corporation or a city council, but the effects of your actions will always be felt outside what you perceive as your immediate sphere. This ripple effect, this interpenetration of levels and fields of influence, means that no mantle of leadership is trivial; every task of leadership works toward the largest ends we can imagine — social justice, peace, health and well-being, a meaningful shared culture.

Now when you add the element of gender to the issues of leadership, a whole specific set of historical circumstances immediately enters the picture. Because political, military, scientific, and artistic leadership of Western European and American societies has for thousands of years been overwhelmingly and often stridently male, the phrase "women in leadership" is by some lights even a contradiction in terms. The woman's role in the patriarchal societies of the West has been to follow, to obey, to support, to provide, but emphatically never to lead, to rule, to decide and dictate. The few women in the past who were leaders — Elizabeth I, Catherine the Great — ruled by virtue of heredity and were exceptions to many rules. In our own century the many women who have played leading roles, particularly in the transformation of the culture of the United States, have had to start from scratch, to create new rules. They have each had to decide to what extent they would adopt the postures and tactics of male leaders and to what extent their action was to be differently based and newly pitched. From the great feminist leaders of the 19th and early 20th centuries to the new generation of highly educated professional women of our time, each one has had to find some new relation to the stereotypes of the past, and each has had a hand in creating new and more energizing stereotypes.

It used to be that women who spoke out, who spoke their minds in public, were punished by being strapped to the ducking stool and submerged in water until they consented to hold their tongues. Or they were muzzled in the town square as a punishment for talking too much or too stridently. They always were expected to be seen, ornamental, but not heard, at least not effectively. In the 19th century women were told that if they persisted in public speaking and politics, their uteruses would dry up — it was politics or progeny, not both.

So consistently have women been distinguished from men in public life that, even today, rhetoric scholar Karlyn Kohrs Campbell can characterize a distinctly "feminine" rhetoric. "Structurally, 'feminine' rhetoric is inductive," she says, "even circuitous, moving from example to example, and is usually grounded in personal experience. Consistent with their allegedly poetic and emotional natures, women tend to adopt associative, dramatic, and narrative modes of development, as opposed to deductive forms of organization. The tone tends to be personal and somewhat tentative, rather than objective and authoritative." So thoroughly have we distinguished between "manly speech" and a feminine style that the televised debate between George Bush and Geraldine Ferraro brought up a whole new set of issues. Interestingly, Bush lost ground at one point by being patronizing, calling his opponent "*Mrs.* Ferraro" instead of Congresswoman Ferraro, and she in turn gained ground by standing up to him. But she also, in woman's historical double-bind, lost some ground with the public, it seems, by relying too much on the factual and combative approach of her law school and courtroom experience and not seeming personal enough.

Each of you will need to decide by your own experience how much and what kind of a factor gender is in leadership and how much power inheres in qualities that are gradually becoming loosened from identification with only one gender. Gender is both a destiny and a decision — it is something we are born into, fated to, with the whole weight of its past and present social pressures. It also is something we each must define, develop, and deploy in a quite individual way, so that it does not inhibit but rather enhances the talents, intelligence, and gifts that we bring.

Biologically there are only two genders, but sociologically and culturally there are many distinguishable shades of masculine and feminine intermixed in endlessly unique ways in the spectrum of individuals. Two eyes, a nose, and a mouth apiece, but an infinite variety of human faces and expressions. Gender is so much more than biology that to reduce it to male and female, its polarity and starting point in the flesh, is barely to begin to understand it. So you will have to keep in the back, or the front, of your minds over the coming days the question of whether this is a conference on "womanly leadership" or a conference on leadership whose participants happen to be women. Is gender an instrument to be used or an obstacle to be overcome or avoided? It is both, of course; but where you lay the emphasis will both define and reveal your own position and what is most important to you.

I would like to offer you two vignettes from one of the remarkable leaders of our time, John F. Kennedy. When asked how he became a hero, a decorated naval hero of the Second World War, he replied, "It was involuntary. They sank my boat." The extraordinary action arises, as often as not, from extremity and apparent disaster — disaster, that is, that someone has the sense and stubborn spirit to make into an opportunity, a chance to rise. When things go wrong, when they get out of control and look like disaster, that is the moment when the leader gets to work. Frustration and failure are not the opposite of leadership but the occasion of it, the ripe time for the new, for giving it all.

The second vignette is a quotation from remarks that Kennedy had prepared to make in Dallas on November 22, 1963, and did not live to deliver. He wrote, "Leadership and learning are indispensable to each other." What a marvelous pair of seeming opposites: leadership, being on top, at the forefront, being effective, making a difference — and learning, being the unknowing but curious one, the searcher and seeker, the questioner looking for an answer. It is learning and the ongoing learning attitude that distinguishes the real leader from the merely momentarily powerful or famous. Just as the strength and potential of people coalesces and becomes visible in a leader, so do their questions and mysteries, their vulnerability and needs, their desire to understand.

I shall leave you with a thought from Susan Brownell Anthony, the Quaker leader of the women's suffrage movement whose image now appears on our coinage. "Cautious, careful people," she said, "always casting about to preserve their reputation and social standing, never can bring about a reform. Those who are really in earnest must be willing to be anything or nothing in the world's estimation." She knew as well as anyone that leadership means risking everything and giving all. It means worrying less about what others think of you and more about the clarity of your own thought and understanding. It means that the reform is the important thing, not the reputation. It means being willing to fail, to go unsung, unthanked, unnoticed.

I am sure you will add a great many more thoughts to these in the coming hours and days. If I may add one word of advice on my own part, it is this: Think hard about leadership and what it means for these few days. Then, when it is over, think harder and longer about the issues that are important to you, the changes you long for and dream of and need. Because leadership is a bit like happiness; it is not something you can simply aim toward or reach out for, but rather something that comes as a by-product of caring passionately and knowledgeably about something, and devoting yourself wholly to that. If you care and then act out of ongoing learning and deep commitment, you will play a leading role, whether you wanted to or not.

The second afternoon to which I invite the reader was an April day, also in 1992, on which I had been asked to address a "Forum of Executive Women" in Philadelphia. I was speaking to professional women on the subject of women as members of boards of trustees, and I used the occasion to order some of my thoughts and experiences of institutional leadership:

When I first begin serving on non-profit boards in the late 1960s and on boards in the profit-making sector in the early 1970s, one could not count on having more than one female or one minority-group colleague, if that, unless it was on the board of a women's school or college. I was — and I felt it — a curiosity to many of the male board members, who often were at least as self-conscious about it all as they were welcoming. It was not quite as bad as Samuel Johnson's remark, "Sir, a woman preaching is like a dog's walking on his hind legs. It is not done well, but you are surprised to find it done at all." His implication, of course, is that it never *can* be done well. But I think that men on boards now generally are relieved and gratified to find that board work and many other kinds of trusteeship and managerial work can indeed be done every bit as well by women as by men. And I think they are happy to find not just the rare exception to act as a token but a growing pool of accomplished female co-workers from among whom they can select the most suitable for their institutional needs.

The growth of a genuine community of women with executive and board experience is, to my mind, one of the most important developments in the women's movement over the last 20 years — years marked by a measure of doubt and dismay on many other fronts. The notion of critical mass is important here in creating and cementing the public perception and acceptance of women's significant presence at all levels of the nation's work life, including and perhaps most especially its boards. Once that perception truly takes hold — that women are both valuable and valued at the top levels of management and public trust — the invisible but palpable "bias barriers" will begin to melt, and gender will eventually come to play very little role in decisions on quality, talent, and fitness to serve.

I am currently serving on the board of one of the nation's largest retail firms, on the board of a banking institution, a telephone company, and an insurance company. I also serve (or have recently served) in the non-profit sector on the boards of several schools and colleges, and many institutes, commissions, and committees. When I joined the board of the retail firm, I received a "position description" — an actual job description of what was expected of a member of their board of directors. Because I had rarely received such a document on joining a board, I suspect that some of you have not received one either, or that you have seen few enough of them to make a brief summary of it of interest here.

The function of the board is, in their words, "to be the primary force pressing the corporation to the realization of its opportunities and fulfillment of its obligations to its shareholders, customers, employees, and the communities in which it operates." To press toward the realization of opportunity and the fulfillment of obligation — good business and good citizenship, profit and partnership, in one sentence, stressing their independence. I thought it was an auspicious beginning.

The responsibilities of the board member were then divided into four categories: planning, organization, operations, and audit. Under planning, the dominant concerns are with the corporate philosophy, the ever-changing environment, long-range goals, standards, policies, plans, and management's performance — in short, the institution's self-definition, the role it conceives for itself. This sort of review and envisioning is work of the kind that appeals to someone who likes to try to understand the contemporary scene at large — locally, nationally, and globally — and who can spend time being concerned about the place of one evolving and complex entity within that larger scheme. This kind of global imagination — its awareness of trends and intuition of possibilities — that I would call "institutional imagination," the ability to see beyond one department or program and to understand the whole corporation is an entity within a much larger field. In providing institutional imagination, the board as a whole acts almost as a collective mind intervening between the institution and its larger context and binding them together, in order to ensure the harmony and fruitful interaction of the two as figure and ground.

The second category, organization, is concerned with management and management succession, organizational strength and manpower planning, benefit policies and practices, and the committees and performance of the board itself. In this case, I would describe what is required as the ability to perceive the inner complexity and dynamic structure of a large thing. Much of that complexity comes from the fact that many of the large numbers refer to people: the quantities are always describing human beings with idiosyncratic talents and common needs. A board member's "leadership sense" — let us call it that, to differentiate it from leadership ability — means not so much his or her own ability to lead others. That type of "leadership sense" is what one exhibits in one's own institution. What one does with "leadership sense" as a board member is to sense how the chemistry and chain reactions of leadership are working down the principal lines of responsibility in the corporation — where the hand is too heavy or too light, whether the managers are being adequately supported and whether they are serving well the goals of the institution.

The third of the board member's responsibilities in the description concerns operations. Its first three words are "review the results." Performance, acquisitions and expenditures, strategies. Given a realistic conception of itself and its goals, and given a positive dynamic of leadership in management, what is happening? What and how is the institution doing? Here again the person with a partisan or departmental imagination will tend to contribute to the inner competition between parts of the institution. Whether he or she is a manager of one manufacturing plant among several or a historian in a university department of history, the departmentalist in most cases has allegiance either limited to a small universe or else spread vastly beyond the institution to a whole field of inquiry or endeavor — particle physics or comparative literature — to which the institution is a means, a contributor. Both of these styles of departmentalism are valid, of course, and necessary to the vitality of research and local functioning of operations. But if the corporation or college is to be well-served, the board member must specialize right in between the partial department and the total universe of inquiry. One must have the ability to become uncommonly interested, on and off, in someone else's business, in order to view it both from a distance and up close in loving and occasionally overwhelming detail. If there is no suspense, excitement, disappointment, or urge to advise, then reviewing the results will be tedious labor indeed.

The final category in the job description, the bottom line, so to speak, is called the "audit." It is interesting to note that this particular position description states that it is the board's responsibility to "be assured that the Board and its committees are adequately and currently informed . . . of the condition of the Corporation and its operations." Within the usual range of fiduciary responsibilities, this corporation asks its board not to assume but to *ensure* that it is being adequately informed. "Audit," of course, means to listen and hear. And we know now that listening is a much more active art than many people have suspected. It requires not so much patience as an ability to sense where the action is, even when it is not quite center stage. The board members individually have to act as the eyes and ears of the institution as a whole: they are a sensory apparatus trained on the corporation or the college from a standpoint which no one else has. Everyone else is either inside the institution or outside it, while the board member is uniquely situated on the edge, with on foot in and one foot out, on purpose and quite indispensably to the institution's welfare. This sort of awareness, the vigilance at the circumference, where the institution verges on its wider community and world, is the first and last resource for institutional integrity, and assurance of honesty to those within and those without, insofar as that is humanly possible.

You will notice, of course, that while we have been considering the functions and responsibilities of the board member, the whole issue of gender has sunk into the background or been reduced to our usual occasional dance of pronouns. We all know that there is nothing in the job description that women cannot do just

163

as well as men. The question before us, and really before the generations of women who are even now being prepared to follow us, is this: Do women in significant numbers truly have the desire and the confidence to aspire to these forms of institutional imagination and leadership sense, this taste for complexity and for listening acutely on behalf of an entity and those with whom and for whom it operates? If they do, it will be because you, we, have helped them to it. And if they do, their warm welcome into the boardrooms of the nation is only a matter of time.

I hope that these two afternoons on the job offer some glimpse of the interesting scenery, the view from one president's office. The fundamental qualification for education leadership, in my view, is a habit of interest in others and a penchant for involvement in complex situations — what Katharine McBride called "a liking for people as they are," and I would add, on behalf of my first and lifelong mentor, "a vision of what they can become."

Rosemary Murray

IN RETROSPECT: DAME ROSEMARY MURRAY
by Karen Doyle Walton

Note: Rather than compose an autobiographical essay, Dame Rosemary Murray asked that I write her profile, drawing on our interviews in 1992 and 1994 and correspondence. I was pleased to be given the privilege to do so.

Dame Rosemary Murray was the founding president of New Hall, Cambridge University. After attending Downe House, a girl's boarding school, Rosemary Murray earned bachelor's and master's degrees from Lady Margaret Hall, Oxford University, followed by B.Sc. and D. Phil. degrees in chemistry. She had two academic posts in chemistry, first at Royal Holloway College (London University) and then at Sheffield University, and during World War II served with the WRNS (Women's Royal Navy Service), earning the rank of Chief Officer.

Returning to academe as assistant lecturer in chemistry at Cambridge University and Fellow of Girton College, she became in 1954 the founding president of New Hall, a new college of Cambridge University, a position from which she retired in 1982. From 1975 to 1977, she also served as the only female vice-chancellor in the history of the university. In addition to being made an Honorary Fellow of Lady Margaret Hall, Oxford, and of Girton, New Hall, and Robinson Colleges, Cambridge, Dame Rosemary has been awarded honorary doctorates from the British universities of Ulster, Leeds, Sheffield, Oxford, and Cambridge, and the University of Pennsylvania, the University of Southern California, and Wellesley College.

To appreciate fully Dame Rosemary Murray's role in the history of Cambridge University, it is helpful to recall the origin of that traditionally masculine institution. Having been described as the "only true university town in England," resting on the banks of the meandering river Cam, Cambridge has, in many ways, defied time for centuries. Records as far back as 1209 recorded the mi-

167

gration of defectors from Oxford University, following disturbances there. Cambridge was already well-established when Pope John XXII officially recognized the University in 1318. Based on the University of Paris model of a collection of colleges under the authority of a central university that grants all degrees, the Statutes of the University document that Cambridge was one of 20 *Studia Generale* in Europe before 1300.

Many college buildings have preserved evidence of the best architects of their respective times. Financed by royal and aristocratic wealth, the colleges were built around rectangles of velvety lawns, which are off-limits to the students, who reside in the chambers surrounding the courtyards and must follow paths around the grass. Only the Master and Fellows who govern each college may set foot on that hallowed ground or sit at high table during the formal candlelight dinners that are still held nightly at some of the ancient colleges in vaulted dining halls lined with portraits of famous graduates. It was not until the 1880s, centuries after the founding of the university, that dons other than heads of the colleges and professors were permitted to marry.

Girton, founded in 1869 to educate women, was deliberately located outside the town. A few years later, Newnham, also for women, was established. Neither was initially a college of Cambridge University; and it was not until 1926 that women were appointed to university posts. Although Girton and Newnham women, in the course of time, were permitted to attend lectures and to complete all requirements, they were not awarded Cambridge University degrees until 1948. In fact, in 1904 the university senate of Trinity College, Dublin, passed a grace (regulation) that permitted women who had fulfilled Cambridge degree requirements to apply for Dublin degrees. During the next 40-plus years, hundreds of women crossed the Irish Sea by ferry the night before Dublin University commencement, paid their graduation fees in the morning, received Dublin University degrees, and then returned immediately to England. These leaders of women's education, who included many who became academic lecturers, teachers, and headmistresses, were known in Trinity College, Dublin, as "steamboat ladies."

I was graciously received by Dame Rosemary on two occasions, in November 1992 and July 1994. She was quite willing to share her life experiences with this American, who at the time of our first meeting was a visiting scholar at Wolfson College, Cambridge, and on the second occasion had just participated in the University of Aberdeen's International Conference on Women in Higher Education.

Consideration of the depth and breadth of Dame Rosemary's background and experience is helpful in understanding the circumstances and sequence of events that preceded her being appointed vice-chancellor of Cambridge. In response to my inquiry about her childhood, Dame Rosemary described her upbringing as the eldest sibling in a family of three girls and three boys as "conventional" for the time. Her father was an admiral in the navy and her mother was the daughter of the head of an Oxford college. Dame Rosemary recalls: ". . . to begin at the beginning, I didn't go to school till I was seven, but by then I could read and write, knew some arithmetic but nothing about 'fractions.' I did know Roman numerals and was very proud when the rest of the class didn't." From the age of thirteen, Dame Rosemary attended Downe House, Newbury, an independent boarding school for girls. As a child, she was always interested in science and was as likely to get a Meccano (erector set) for Christmas as a doll. After secondary school, Dame Rosemary earned a B.A. degree in chemistry in 1934 from Lady Margaret Hall, an Oxford women's college, followed by an Oxford D. Phil. in the same field.

Dame Rosemary's Oxbridge roots can be traced to her grandfather William A. Spooner, warden of New College, Oxford, in the early 1900s, whose penchant for accidentally transposing the first letters of two words (as in *tons of soil* for *sons of toil*) gave rise to the term "spoonerism." She related that Dr. Spooner's only son attended college, but none of his daughters (including Dame Rosemary's mother) did so, despite the fact that Spooner was vice chairman of Lady Margaret Hall in 1910, at the time when her mother was the appropriate age to attend. However, Dame Rosemary herself was encouraged by her parents to pursue higher education.

Dame Rosemary's first academic post after leaving Oxford was as a demonstrator in chemistry (equivalent to assistant lecturer) at Royal Holloway College, a women's college of London University. There were three members of staff for chemistry, Dame Rosemary, a professor, and a lecturer, who together covered the whole syllabus for an honors degree in chemistry.

When war was declared in September 1939, Dame Rosemary was living in her family's home near Portsmouth. At first they had children billeted in the house who were evacuees from London. Subsequently their house was requisitioned by the army, except for three rooms and a kitchen, in which her family remained throughout the war. At the time of Dunkirk in 1940, Dame Rosemary was doing research in chemistry at Oxford. During university vacation, she signed on as a part-time volunteer ambulance driver and spent hours trying to learn how to back a car with a trailer (to carry stretchers). However, she admits, "This I never really mastered!"

Early in 1941 she was released from her post at Royal Holloway College and was working as a scientific civil servant at the naval Signal School in Portsmouth at the time of the sinking of the *Bismarck,* which was one of the first occasions on which radar was of value to the navy. However, she was not using her qualifications as a chemist; and so when she was offered a job at Sheffield University, she felt she should take it. But after a year, she found the work to be very frustrating. Thus on Trafalgar Day, 21 October 1942, she joined the WRNS (Women's Royal Naval Service) as a wren rating — the lowest rank — having refused a commission to enter as an officer. The six months she was a wren were spent in London at Westfield College (where eight women slept in a tutor's room in bunkbeds), at Chatham, and in the Midlands. She was then selected for a commission, went to the WRNS OTC (Officers Training Corps) at Greenwich Royal Naval College, and was posted as a third officer to the navy base at Londonderry, where 600 wrens were doing all manner of jobs. Writers, coders, teleprinter operators, cooks, stewards, and technicians worked at the naval base and on the ships that came in from convoy duty.

After a period as second officer, she was promoted and was posted to London as a first officer to WRNS headquarters to appoint wren officers. After promotion to chief officer, Dame Rosemary moved to Scotland to the Fleet Air Arm and finally became the WRNS drafting officer at Chatham. This was after the end of the war, and her main work was demobilization of wrens. "We had an enormous index of some 20,000 cards of wrens in the Nore Command. I began to suspect that there were more cards than bodies and then we found that during the war every time a wren had got married a new card had been made out under her married name but the old card had not been removed nor cross-referenced. That took some sorting out."

Dame Rosemary returned to academe after the war:

> One morning at Chatham in 1946, I received a telegram from the mistress of Girton College, one of the two Cambridge women's colleges at the time, asking if I would like to come to interview for a post as chemist. Although I had not considered what I would do after the war, this seemed too good an opportunity to miss, so off I went in wren uniform to Cambridge and had various interviews and was shown the chemistry laboratories by the professor. I gathered later that I caused quite a stir among the technicians — a wren officer in uniform going round the chemistry lab.

She was appointed college lecturer in chemistry at Girton at a salary of about £200 per annum plus residence. Initially, Dame Rosemary found returning to teaching and research in chemistry to be difficult after four years in the navy. However, her varied experiences during that hiatus from academe proved applicable to many of the new challenges that Cambridge presented.

In 1946, Cambridge considered the status of women in the university. In her history of New Hall, *New Hall, 1954-1972: The Making of a College* (Cambridge University Library, 1980), Dame Rosemary describes the Cambridge Council of the Senate deliberations concerning whether women should be recognized as members of the university. A syndicate appointed by the council in 1947 recommended that women should be admitted as members of the university with a limitation on numbers:

> The report was discussed in the usual way; the only speaker at the discussion, Professor Dickins, opposed the recommendations. He stated that women had no substantial grievances and asked how women would be benefited; Oxford had taken the same step a generation ago and Oxford was not particularly happy about it; women were no better treated in Oxford, they had the shadow of power but no more substance than before; no woman had been appointed to a Chair; Cambridge should stand with all male Universities, like Harvard and Yale, rather than with Oxford. On 9th December 1947 the Grace approving the admission of women as members of the University was passed with no opposition. The amendment of Statute was approved by The King in Council in April 1948. And there on the University side the matter rested.

Girton and Newnham were given college status, and subsequently all of the men's colleges admitted women as students and fellows. Girton College now accepts men as well as women, and only Newnham College, New Hall, and Lucy Cavendish remain restricted to women students.

When Dame Rosemary became a demonstrator in chemistry in the university in 1947, she was the first woman to be so appointed. In 1948, the Queen (now the Queen Mother) became the first woman to receive a Cambridge degree, an honorary Doctor of Laws. When the students of Girton and Newnham became members of the university, there was only one woman undergraduate for every eleven men. The Third Foundation Association was formed to seek ways of increasing this number; and after two or three years it was decided to start a new college for women, which eventually became New Hall. Various people suggested that Dame Rosemary apply for the post of Tutor in Charge, and she was appointed.

The opening of New Hall in October was heralded by an article in the *Times Educational Supplement* of 24 September 1954:

In October a third society for women, New Hall, will open its doors for its first 16 undergraduates; and so quickly do old controversies die, it seems entirely natural and proper that it should. In fact its appearance may be thought overdue; Oxford has five colleges for women and about 1,000 women students; New Hall will bring up Cambridge's score to three and may soon increase the number of women students at the University, which is now about 700.

Additional notices about the new Cambridge college for women appeared in several European papers and as far afield as in the *Iraq Times*, the *Rhodesia Herald,* and the *Cairo Times.*

New Hall opened with only two senior members, 15 students, and no funding from the university benefactors or the government. When the first students arrived at the Hermitage, a large manse on Silver Street that had been a guest house, each room had a bed, a table or desk, a chair, a bookcase, somewhere to keep clothes (chest of drawers and hanging cupboard) and a towel rail. As money was scarce, most of the furniture was secondhand. Some of the tables that Dame Rosemary made out of old washstands by covering them with white hardboard can still be found in New Hall students' rooms.

Dame Rosemary recalls, "When the first undergraduates arrived they drew lots for rooms and the tallest among them got the smallest room; her towel rail had to be on the outside of her door." Dame Rosemary's hands-on style as tutor of New Hall also was evidenced by her personally carrying out such jobs as corresponding with the first undergraduates, interviewing all applicants, establishing student records, setting up accounts, and supervising students in chemistry. She recollects, "New Hall began in a house with a small garden going down to the river Cam and with a magnificent pear tree of 50 or 60 feet in the middle of a lawn. As there was no gardener, I also looked after the garden. Some years later, when the undergraduates made use of the river frontage by having a punt [boat], I added 'boatkeeper' and maintenance of the punt to my activities."

On 28 June 1972, Her Majesty in Council approved the grant of a Charter of Incorporation to New Hall under the name and style of "The President and Fellows of New Hall in the University of Cambridge," and New Hall became a college of the university. The founding and nurturing of New Hall was a labor of devotion that Dame Rosemary found to be hard work, but not worrisome. She reserved Sundays for relaxing by gardening and bookbinding, the latter being a hobby that combined the practical with the aesthetic.

The chancellor of Cambridge University is the Duke of Edinburgh. Whereas the chancellor of a British university is an honorary position, it is the vice-chancellor who is the executive head and chairs the committees that determine university policy. In Cambridge, the vice-chancellor is chosen from the heads of the colleges and serves for two years. (This age-old practice recently has been amended.) After 21 years as head of New Hall and serving on numerous university committees, Dame Rosemary was elected vice-chancellor of Cambridge and served from 1975 to 1977. Since the establishment of the post of vice-chancellor in 1412, 341 men and only one woman have held that position.

When asked about whether she attributed her leadership ability to innate talent or acquired skills, Dame Rosemary deflected the question with characteristic gentility. But surely her war experience as a wren provided opportunities to practice and develop administrative and management techniques based on her native instincts. My question concerning her assuming the role of figurehead for a Cambridge college elicited Dame Rosemary's response that on her arrival at Girton College after the war, she was "very shy and apprehensive" when asked to give speeches and award prizes. However, the self-confidence she has clearly developed through experience is now evident in her comfortable poise.

Although Dame Rosemary did not have a mentor at Oxford to support her pursuit of a doctorate in chemistry, she has served as mentor and role model for other women, whom she has encouraged to take active roles in college and university committee work. For example, Dr. Kate Pretty, president of Homerton College,

174

Cambridge, who earned her undergraduate degree at New Hall, acknowledges her gratitude and appreciation of Dame Rosemary's guidance. And despite her military experience, Dame Rosemary leads by example, rather than by giving commands. With unflappable demeanor, she listens to her subordinates, encouraging them and enabling them to know their worth.

Dame Rosemary does not acknowledge experiencing active opposition to her assuming roles unusual for a woman at a male-dominated institution that is generally considered the greatest scientific university in the country. However, her appointment as the first female vice-chancellor was not welcomed by all: "When I became vice-chancellor, one of the heads of the colleges was very dubious. But he was polite enough never to say so to my face."

Dame Rosemary's numerous other leadership roles reflect her wide range of interests. She has been the president of the National Association of Adult Education, the first woman director of a British bank, the first woman liveryman of the prestigious Goldsmith Company, and the only woman on the Armed Forces Pay Review Body. Her national and international recognitions include honorary degrees from the British universities of Ulster, Leeds, Sheffield, Oxford, and Cambridge, and in the United States from Wellesley College, the University of Pennsylvania, and the University of Southern California.

When asked to look back at her life in the comfort and tranquillity of her Cambridge living room in 1994, Dame Rosemary reflected modestly, "I have had an unusual career. I've just been very fortunate." No air of grandeur is even vaguely perceptible in the person of Dame Rosemary Murray, a handsome, gracious woman to whom self-aggrandizement and pomp are totally foreign. But her presence is formidable. I realized during my two inspiring visits that I was witnessing a remarkable woman whose influence continues through the accomplishments of generations of New Hall alumnae.

Diana Natalicio

LIFE IS A
TEAM SPORT
by Diana Natalicio

Diana Natalicio is the president of the University of Texas at El Paso.
She received her B.S. in Spanish summa cum laude *from St. Louis Uni-*
versity and a master's in Portuguese and a Ph.D. in Linguistics from
the University of Texas at Austin. She was a Fulbright scholar in Rio de
Janeiro, Brazil, and a visiting scholar in Lisbon, Portugal. Before be-
coming president of the University of Texas at El Paso, Dr. Natalicio
served as chair of Modern Languages, dean of Liberal Arts, and vice
president for Academic Affairs at that institution.

She has written numerous books, monographs, and articles in the field
of applied linguistics. Her public and professional service has included
membership on the NASA Advisory Council and the Fogarty Interna-
tional Center at the National Institutes of Health, and on the boards of
the U.S.-Mexico Commission for Educational and Cultural Exchange
(Fulbright-Garcia Robles), the Fund for the Improvement of Post-Sec-
ondary Education (FIPSE), the National Action Council for Minorities
in Engineering (NACME), and the American Association for Higher
Education (AAHE board of directors chair, 1995). Dr. Natalicio also
was appointed by President George Bush to the Commission for Edu-
cational Excellence of Hispanic Americans and by President Bill Clin-
ton to the National Science Board.

Memories of my childhood, of growing up in St. Louis, Missouri, in the 1940s, are all happy. In fact, I would be hard-pressed
to recall an unpleasant event. Life then was stable, comfortable,
and carefree.

I loved school, and I can remember only one teacher in all of
my elementary school years that I really did not like. I liked my
teachers so much, in fact, that I wanted to be one, and I often
organized my dolls and my friends in classes so that I could teach
them everything from reading to piano. I also remember playing.

My brother and I and other boys in the neighborhood — there weren't many girls on my block — played regularly and with gusto. We played basketball on a hoop that my father fixed to the back of the garage in the alley, we roller-skated on the sidewalks around the block and through alleys, we went exploring, fishing, and ice skating in the park across the street, and, most of all, we played baseball.

I loved baseball, and deep down inside I wanted to be a baseball player even more than I wanted to be a teacher. Although I was a good pitcher — certainly as good as the boys — I watched as the boys were encouraged to play in leagues and on varsity teams and the girls became cheerleaders and fans. That was when I first understood that wanting to do something and being good at it, though important, were not sufficient conditions for success. I understood that others had to do their part to create opportunities, and they didn't do that for me in baseball.

High school in the 1950s was generally happy, though like most of my peers, I struggled with adolescence. But the 1950s were simple times, and whatever peer pressures I felt were balanced by the very real social constraints that governed my and my friends' behavior.

My recollections of high school revolve far more around a social calendar than on meaningful academic experiences. With only a couple of exceptions, my high school teachers remain faceless and nameless in mental storage. Like most adolescents in the 1950s, I enjoyed dances, parties, and being with friends; and high school served as a convenient meeting point to ensure that such activities were planned and carried out. Mine was a blue-collar, public high school, where most students had little or no aspiration for postsecondary education. At that time, all of us could anticipate getting a good job after high school with little or no difficulty.

When I graduated from high school at mid-year, I secured a job as a secretary-receptionist at a large manufacturing firm in St. Louis. The shorthand and typing skills I acquired in high school at my father's urging — he had once worked as an office assistant — were the key to my success in securing this position, and

I enjoyed the work. I also enjoyed the paychecks that I initially used to buy a car and some clothes. However, as the months rolled on and September grew nearer, I began to question the wisdom of my original objective to work full-time only until the beginning of the academic year. Neither one of my parents had attended college, and most of my friends would not do so either. The decision to go to college therefore was not natural, simply because I had no role models or peer pressure to help me along. The one question that seems to have made a difference for me was: "Do I want to do this job, however much I like it now, for the rest of my life?" My answer was, "I don't think so."

On that somewhat flimsy pretext, I enrolled at St. Louis University; at that time, there was no public university in St. Louis. Very quickly, I realized that my high school preparation was inadequate to enable me to compete with my fellow St. Louis University students. Continuing to work part-time as a secretary and extraordinarily challenged by the academic demands placed before me, I had no choice but to work very hard and almost nonstop. Although others at St. Louis University may have been busy with social organizations and activities, I participated in none. I was a commuter student who, like many of the "nontraditional" students that I know and work with at the University of Texas at El Paso (UTEP) today, had only limited contact with the university beyond the classroom. Although I did not use the formal support mechanisms made available to me, I was regularly encouraged and given special attention by faculty members who informally communicated to me the importance of my academic success. And I did succeed, graduating *summa cum laude* from St. Louis University in the then-traditional four-year time span while, not so traditionally, continuing to work at secretarial and tutoring jobs.

One vivid memory of my college years was the sheer terror that I felt whenever I thought I might be required to speak up in class. I did my best to avoid eye contact with any professor in the act of posing questions to a class, even when I was sure that I knew the answer; and I never volunteered to respond to a profes-

179

sor's call for questions or comments. In part, my fear of speaking up surely related to a lack of confidence in my academic preparation for college. In larger measure, however, it reflected a determination never to suffer the embarrassment of a public mistake. Although I had reluctantly accepted the notion that I was capable of making an error now and then, I was not yet willing to share my flaws with others.

One of my degree requirements at St. Louis University was a course in oral interpretation of literature. I could have elected to enroll in a public speaking course instead, but I decided that reading someone else's work to my fellow students might be slightly less terrifying than presenting my own remarks. Needless to say, I was not the star of my oral interpretation class. While other students brought us to tears with their emotional presentations, the only tears that I stimulated during my performances were my own. Oral interpretation of literature was without a doubt the most difficult — and dreaded — course in my degree plan.

During my senior year at the university, I was encouraged to pursue postgraduate education. I was provided information on fellowship opportunities and technical assistance in preparing my applications. One of the fellowships that I applied for was a Fulbright to Brazil, primarily because one of my Spanish professors had taught a course in Portuguese language. At the time that I sent off the application, I believed that I had little or no chance of being awarded this fellowship. When some months later I received a letter informing me that I had, in fact, been selected for the Fulbright, I was absolutely terrified. I had never flown on an airplane nor had I ever lived away from home; and a Fulbright to Brazil required that I do both. For two days I carried the letter with me without divulging its contents to anyone, convinced that I could decline this opportunity so discreetly that no one would ever know that I had done so. Still, after a couple of days of grappling with my apprehension, I decided not only to go public with the news but to go to Brazil.

I had many second thoughts during the months prior to my departure, but I steadfastly began preparations for the adventure.

On the appointed day, I vividly recall the moment when my flight was called at the St. Louis airport, hugging my parents, and beginning the long walk across the tarmac — there were no jetways in those days — to the airplane. My knees buckled, partly because I had crammed into two carry-on bags an enormous collection of items that I assumed would be unavailable in Brazil, and partly out of fear of the unknown world I was about to enter. I recall thinking as I walked toward the plane that I could easily do an about-face and return to the terminal and to the more predictable life that I knew. But I chose to proceed, to depart for what would become the most educationally enriching and personally satisfying year of my life.

Brazil offered me staggering opportunities for personal and professional growth. I traveled widely, absorbing language and culture in intoxicating doses, and I was overwhelmed by the beauty of the country and the openness of its people. Perhaps the most important lesson I learned, however, was how to escape from the public perfection model I had imposed on myself, to enjoy myself, and even to laugh at myself. But to be totally honest, I can claim no credit for this major accomplishment; instead, it was the direct result of my limited knowledge of spoken Portuguese.

I had studied both Spanish and Portuguese in college; but like far too many foreign language students, I learned to read well, to write and understand some, and to speak very little. When I arrived at the airport in Rio de Janeiro to begin my Fulbright year, I was struck by how little of the Portuguese spoken by Brazilians was even minimally intelligible to me. For a moment I panicked, thinking that my first airplane ride had taken me to an unintended destination; my only reassurance was the company of fellow Fulbrighters, at least some of whom had prior travel experience. During the first couple of weeks in Brazil, I said very little, for to have done so would have required that I risk the embarrassment of saying something — nearly everything — wrong.

When after a few days all the other Fulbrighters in my group left for Sao Paulo, I remained alone in Rio de Janeiro, and the communication crutch that I had relied on — speaking English to them — went with them. I then realized that if I did not begin to speak Portuguese, I would spend a year in silence. I also understood for the first time that making and correcting errors was an effective language learning strategy, and I discovered that making a public mistake was not as painful as I had imagined. In fact, the Brazilians were not only patient and understanding of my language challenges, they were enormously supportive. They rarely laughed at my efforts, and they gave me the confidence I so greatly needed to keep talking until I got it right. Within six months, my self-confidence had risen significantly, and I was learning Portuguese faster and more enjoyably than I had ever dreamed possible. I loved the Portuguese language and the window that it gave me into Brazilian life and culture; I loved learning it by talking and listening to Brazilians; and I even enjoyed making mistakes.

After returning from Brazil, I spent most of the decade of the 1960s as a graduate student at the University of Texas at Austin, not so much by design as by the good fortune of being in Rio de Janeiro when the director of the Portuguese program traveled there to recruit graduate student teaching assistants. Graduate school and Austin were extraordinarily good places to be in the 1960s, and I enjoyed both my master's degree program in Portuguese and, especially, my doctoral program in linguistics. I also spent 18 months as a Gulbenkian Foundation Fellow in Portugal during that period, and that experience taught me a great deal about the world, the diversity of its peoples and cultures, and about my capacity to meet the challenges of an ever-changing context.

I worked as a teaching assistant in introductory Portuguese while completing a master's degree in Portuguese language and Brazilian area studies at UT Austin. I enjoyed teaching very much, and I especially enjoyed the challenge of trying to simulate for students my language learning experiences in Brazil. I focused on speaking and listening skills and brought to the classroom all manner of artifacts, music, and books that I had collected while there. I derived as much satisfaction from my students' progress in Portuguese as I had from my own, and I experimented with a wide variety of teaching strategies to make the language come alive for them.

But I enjoyed my master's degree work less. The literature that I had devoured while in Brazil lost its luster under the scrutiny of literary analysis. Dissecting my favorite Brazilian novels destroyed their soul and doused my passion. I was restless.

I departed for Europe as soon as my master's degree work was completed, and for the next 18 months I tried to work as an independent researcher in what was then a hostile environment for researchers. In the waning years of the Salazar regime, Portugal was desperately clinging to such "overseas provinces" as Angola and Mozambique, while at the same time trying to maintain tight control over its citizens at home. Foreigners were viewed with suspicion, and a restless American researcher was hardly a welcome visitor. Although my fellowship from a Portuguese foundation granted me 12 months of support, the only visa I was able to secure was a 60-day tourist variety. At the end of the first 60 days, I tried to extend the visa; but I was told that it was not renewable, and I learned from non-official sources that the way around this common problem for foreign visitors was to leave the country and return with another 60-day tourist visa that would be readily granted at the border. Thus for the remainder of my stay, I had a totally legitimate excuse to travel regularly to Spain or elsewhere in Europe. Although such trips were enjoyable and educational, they certainly disrupted my research agenda.

I also hoped to travel to the overseas provinces, particularly Mozambique, to learn more about the Portuguese language and literature there. However, in spite of numerous and tenacious efforts, I never succeeded in securing authorization for that visit. Instead, I was offered the opportunity to travel to the Cape Verde Islands, a province that at the time was far more peaceful and, in retrospect, probably far more conducive to research than Mozambique.

I spent several weeks in the Cape Verde Islands. Although initially disappointed at the compromise on my destination, I was immediately intrigued by the Creole language spoken on the islands; and I began to try to decipher its structure. I had no formal training in linguistics at that time, but I began to develop my own set of analytical tools and descriptive techniques. I returned to Portugal determined to learn more about language analysis. That opportunity presented itself when, shortly after arriving in Lisbon, I received a letter from a former graduate student colleague in Austin, who encouraged me to return to the University of Texas to pursue a Ph.D. in linguistics.

My first year of linguistic study was tremendously exciting. The field was in transition: Structuralism was struggling, and Noam Chomsky's transformational grammar was gaining adherents. The UT Austin Linguistics Department was a mix of both camps, and the tensions between them created an exhilarating environment for the graduate students fortunate enough to be there at the time. We were all caught up in the excitement of serving as warriors in the linguistic revolution, and linguistics became a new passion for me.

I had a National Defense Education Act fellowship for my doctoral studies and so did not teach. However, a splendid language teaching opportunity arose one summer when I served as language coordinator for a Peace Corps training program conducted just outside of Rio de Janeiro in Brazil. In-country training programs for Peace Corps volunteers were experimental at that time, and I was given enormous latitude to develop a program to fit the setting. This could not have been a more satisfying assignment. In addition, it was in this setting that I learned for the first time that I enjoyed management duties almost as much as I enjoyed teaching.

After a short stint working as a research associate at UT Austin after completing my doctorate, I reluctantly realized that I would have to leave Austin to pursue an academic career. I accepted the offer of a faculty position at the University of Texas at El Paso (UTEP) with some trepidation, for I had never been to El Paso and most people I knew in Austin reacted as if I were headed for the last stop on the stage coach line to nowhere. Of course, they had never been to El Paso either. But, like my decision to go to Brazil as a Fulbright student, accepting a faculty position at UTEP turned out to be an extraordinarily fortuitous step in my life.

It did not seem so in the beginning. The desert terrain struck me as harsh; and just as I questioned my sanity on several occasions during the first few weeks I was in Brazil, I also wondered whether El Paso was really the right place for me. However, I quickly learned that the opportunities at UTEP were truly extraordinary and that the people on the campus and in the community were the best I had ever encountered anywhere. I also loved living in the bilingual, binational metropolitan area of El Paso-Juarez. And the Southwest mountain and desert environments totally captivated me.

After a couple of years as a faculty member in linguistics, I was invited to serve as interim department chair in the Modern Languages Department, not because I was eminently qualified for the position but, as a newcomer with a joint appointment in linguistics, I apparently was the only politically neutral faculty member in the department. Like most faculty members who assume their first administrative position, I expressed an appropriate disdain for the chair's role and vigorously asserted that my tenure as an administrator would be short.

The department chairmanship led to an invitation to serve as associate dean of the College of Liberal Arts. My pretense of disliking administrative work grew fragile when I accepted this position. I rounded up the usual excuses — "it's an opportunity to learn," "I'll only do it for a short while" — but the truth was that I enjoyed administrative work.

The one aspect of administrative work that I did not like was public speaking. As I was called on in my new role in the dean's office to welcome groups to the college or to make other public statements, I experienced the same fear that had inhibited me from participating in class during college. Even brief "welcome to UTEP" remarks were a source of tremendous anxiety. I would write every word on a card prior to the event and read it, rather than utter something embarrassing while attempting to speak extemporaneously. It was perhaps at this juncture in my life that I fully understood this critical gap in my preparation.

As I talk with UTEP students today, I always encourage them to take every opportunity available to develop their communication skills, both oral and written. It is interesting, I think, that we

185

seem far more concerned about written communication skills in our precollegiate and postsecondary curricula, when oral communication plays such a major role in all of our lives. Stage fright is surprisingly common among professionals I know, especially women; and having endured my own bout with it, I now urge every young person to seek opportunities for oral language practice. It is far easier to acquire these skills as a student than it is to suffer abdominal cramps before welcoming even a small group as dean of the College of Liberal Arts or vice president for academic affairs. As I speak frequently and extemporaneously to large audiences today, I am both astonished — and relieved — at how truly easy it has become to do what was unthinkable ten years ago.

I am often asked how I planned my administrative career. My response is that I did not have a precise plan. The fact is that I have always enjoyed my work immensely, and I have found each assignment an exciting opportunity to grow in new directions. I liked being department chair, I enjoyed being associate dean and dean of the College of Liberal Arts, and I found the vice presidency for academic affairs enormously challenging.

I also am told that it is unusual to proceed through a variety of administrative ranks at the same institution — that it is far more common to move out in order to move up. That option never occurred to me. I loved El Paso, the Southwest generally, and UTEP in particular. I have always been excited by the mission of this institution and the critical role that it plays in fostering the human and economic development of this historically underserved border region. I love being on an international boundary in a bilingual/bicultural area, and the vicarious pleasure that I derive from participating in the success of the talented and eager students served by UTEP provides all of the emotional awards that I could ever hope for. I have never viewed what I do at UTEP as merely a job; it is a passion.

I sometimes am asked whether being a woman president presents special challenges to me. In general, my response is that it doesn't seem to make all that much difference. Legislative hearings present me with the same questions and challenges that are imposed on my male colleagues; students deflate any tendency toward ego inflation with their disarming questions and feedback; faculty members consider me just as addled as my male colleagues who have chosen an administrative career; and athletic boosters consider me and my male colleagues hopelessly inept when our teams lose and only marginally acceptable when they win. It is obvious that women still represent a small minority of university presidents and that there continue to be those faculty, students, and alumni who are not totally comfortable with the idea of a woman executive. My strategy in dealing with this attitude is to ignore it. During the seven years that I have been president, I believe that I have changed more attitudes by doing my job well than by worrying about or debating those attitudes.

I struggled with this autobiographical assignment and nearly decided not to complete it, because my story is not really "mine." Instead, it reflects the partnership that I have enjoyed with a host of individuals who created for me opportunities for personal and professional growth and development: my parents, who ensured that my childhood was secure and happy; an aunt and uncle who taught me to love books and to appreciate nature; a brother who provoked me into becoming a better baseball pitcher than he; teachers, especially the Jesuits at St. Louis University, who taught me to think and to love learning; the Fulbright program that launched me from my stable home and familiar neighborhood into a world of boundless diversity and challenge; friends who generously shared their knowledge and advice; and the UTEP students, faculty, and staff and members of the El Paso community, who have given me the extraordinary privilege of serving as UTEP's president. To be sure, I have worked — often very hard — to capitalize on opportunities presented to me, and I have been willing to take significant personal and professional risks. But without those partners and the opportunities that they have created for me, there would have been no story to tell.

Pauline Perry

HAPPY IS MY LOT
by Pauline Perry

Baroness Pauline Perry is the president of Lucy Cavendish College, Cambridge University. She read moral sciences (philosophy) at Girton College, Cambridge University, and then taught philosophy at American and Canadian universities for approximately ten years. After returning to England, Baroness Perry published extensively in education journals, authored three textbooks, and was a journalist for newspapers, radio, and television.

During her 17-year career with Her Majesty's Inspectorate of Schools, she assumed the posts of chief inspector and the Secretary of State's professional adviser on higher education and teacher training. In 1987, she was appointed the first woman in the United Kingdom to head a polytechnic, later to become South Bank University. During her seven years there, the enrollment grew from 10,000 in 1986 to 20,000 in 1993. Her leadership in educational and civic organizations has been recognized by the awarding of honorary degrees from the Universities of Bath, Sussex, Aberdeen, Wolverhampton, Surrey, and South Bank. She was made a Life Peer, a member of the House of Lords, in 1991. In 1994, the Right Honorable Baroness Perry of Southwark took up the post of president of Lucy Cavendish College.

Education has always seemed to me to be the most natural and obvious choice for my career. Although I cannot recall ever having any plan or well thought out goal for the work that I would do, nevertheless when the opportunity came to me after years of child rearing to start on a serious career of my own, the first thought that came to my mind was that I should teach.

Like many women of my generation, I married very soon after graduation (six weeks exactly from receiving my degree in Cambridge University's Senate House) and immediately followed my husband's career, which at that time took him to the United States of America. I cannot remember any serious debate with myself about the implications for my career of getting married so young

(I was 20 at the time), nor any real understanding of what the social climate of the time expected of women, educated or otherwise. All I knew was that I was very much in love, excited at the prospect of traveling to the west coast of North America, and extremely busy both planning my wedding and preparing for my Cambridge finals.

In retrospect, perhaps one of the oddest things about that period of my life is that I expected, without question, that I would be able to continue with my academic study after marriage without anything other than a location change. Indeed, on arrival in Seattle I registered as a Ph.D. student at the University of Washington and was successful in receiving an appointment as a graduate assistant in the Philosophy Department. (In the University of Washington, graduate assistants took the title of *reader*, which greatly amused my Cambridge friends.) However, the assumptions I had made were overly optimistic, at least in respect of my academic aspirations. I became pregnant within two months with my first child, who was born one year to the day from the date of my receiving my Cambridge degree.

In total I had 11 years of delay in starting my full-time career, over the period when I was fully engaged in the rearing of my four children. During those years I worked hard to maintain some kind of professional identity, not because I had any coherent career plan but more to provide some kind of stimulus for my own mind and as a contrast to the responsibilities of home and children.

It is all too easy to complain that the interruption of women's careers resulting from family responsibility is wholly a disadvantage. It also has many advantages not available to men who, at least in the generation of which I was a member, tended to accept that their responsibility for providing the family income overrode any wish to pursue eccentric hobbies or interests as they might wish. Conversely, I was able during those years to take on several activities that I greatly enjoyed and that gave me a range of experience that would have been impossible alongside a full-time career. With much enthusiasm I worked as a freelance journalist, using a battered portable typewriter in the family dining room and writing articles, broadcasts for radio and television, and a weekly column in the *Oxford Mail* during the odd intervals when the children were at school or asleep.

It also was during this period that I had my first introduction to the field of adult education, which I still believe is one of the most exciting and rewarding areas of the whole education spectrum. In Massachusetts, I enjoyed sharing my less-than-perfect knowledge of French with an enthusiastic group of learners, some of whom were motivated by the search for their own cultural roots in France. This experience I found as stimulating as the more academically demanding experience of teaching postgraduate philosophy to part-time students on Saturday mornings and in the late evenings for the University of Massachusetts. I was a part-time lecturer to a largely adult group of students in the University of Manitoba and even taught English as a foreign language in Saskatchewan to evening-class students who came from a rich and varied range of national backgrounds.

One might call that decade of experience a rag bag or mishmash, but over the years it has proved an invaluable source of experience and personal learning on which to base a later full-time career. As journalist, broadcaster, and adult educator, I developed a depth of understanding of the wider community and of the needs of adult readers, listeners, and learners, which would have been impossible to acquire in a more conventional type of employment. Combining it, inevitably, with the demands of housework and children forced me to develop a rigid structure of time management, which has stood me in unbelievably good stead in later years, as I have continued to try to fit 30 hours into every day.

When I was ready to take up a full-time career, with my children more or less launched into full-time schooling, I was surprised and pleased to find that my "rag bag" of experience gave me some credibility in achieving a full-time post in my early thirties, as lecturer in charge of one of the first access courses for mature women to enter teacher training in the University of Oxford's Associated Colleges of Education. I have enormously affectionate memories of four successive years of running the one-year course and am pleased and proud to see the success that many of those women have achieved in their careers. Working with them was an immensely exciting and rewarding experience. They were highly motivated, often exceptionally intelligent, and exhibited a degree of mutual support and encouragement for one another which was a genuine inspiration.

Four years and three published books later, I became one of Her Majesty's inspectors of schools with what was then called the Department of Education and Science; and from then until 1944, I worked in a world where women were in a tiny minority. While working in this predominantly male world, I occasionally used to reflect on the fact that I was educated at an all-girls' school from the age of six, spent my undergraduate years at Girton College in Cambridge at a time when it was an all-female college, and for many years was a housewife in the company of other women with small children in the enclosed world of what Marilyn French has called "the women's room." I have found this to be a strength rather than a weakness. Many years of the supportive friendship of other women has been a very solid rock on which to stand in a world where men predominated and in which later I found myself first as chief inspector in Her Majesty's Inspectorate, and later as head of an institution where men were overwhelmingly in the majority.

It was in the Inspectorate that I met what I suppose was the first female mentor of my professional life, though the official mentor I was given was a man and a very dear and kind man at that. It was Sheila Browne, at the time I joined the Inspectorate, who seemed to me to be the most exciting thinker and therefore the person I most wished to know better in the whole of the Inspectorate hierarchy. At the time she was a staff inspector and had two more promotions to go before becoming senior chief inspector; nevertheless, she already was beginning to influence some of the younger and newer members among us. We preferred her vision of an Inspectorate that would use its huge experience of the day-to-day life of colleges and schools to inform the processes of ministerial policy making, above the rather cozy image of the Inspectorate as a body who popped in and out of schools giving wise advice to head teachers, which was then the prevailing view.

It was Sheila Browne who, after becoming senior chief inspector, promoted me to staff inspector and later to chief inspector, with all the national responsibility and giving of quality advice which that role incurred. It also gave me my first real experience of "management."

The task of both staff inspectors and chief inspectors within the department is a fascinating one. Standing as the link between a large body of highly expert professionals, who are evaluating and assessing the work of educational institutions, and the policy makers of the government department and ministers themselves, one is in a very influential position. Civil servants can advise ministers on the legal and administrative consequences of policy options, and they are exceptionally intelligent and experienced government servants whose expertise is a constant source of financial and administrative wisdom in the workings of government. However, those of us who were professional advisors had a very special role to play in the advice to ministers; and the strength of HM inspectors lay in their firsthand information and knowledge of educational practice.

Although contact with politicians confirmed my personal feelings that I had no reason to envy them the pressures and confrontational nature of their job, it was possible to learn much from watching the way these highly motivated and ambitious people conduct their lives. Seeing people as diverse as Margaret Thatcher, Shirley Williams, Keith Joseph, or Kenneth Baker attacking the education issues that they saw of paramount importance was a fascinating and educational experience. Although their personalities were very different, they shared one characteristic: an ability to concentrate entirely on the issue at hand, to identify the one or two really important issues out of a plethora of detail, and to devote their energy to those. They also shared an ability to remain remarkably calm under pressures political or personal.

I also owe a great debt to the senior civil servants, with whom I felt myself most privileged to work. The civil servants of the generation now in their forties and fifties were without question the cream of their graduate contemporaries, as in the 1960s and 1970s entering the administrative grades of the Civil Service was considered one of the more desirable careers for the high attainers. They had quick minds, high analytic ability, and above all an ability to write fast, under pressure, in clear and often elegant prose. From their writing I learned a great deal about the skills of expressing ideas succinctly and presenting arguments in a way that was both neutral and fair, as all who work for ministers are required to do in contributing to the policy debate. I found my years of freelance journalism stood me in good stead, insofar as they had trained me to write to deadlines; but it goes without saying that the change in style required was itself decidedly challenging.

Despite the overall male character of the Department of Education and Science at the time I served there, I was aware of any real prejudice against women only from the occasional individual. By and large, the Civil Service rewards those who deliver, regardless of gender; and the opportunities for favoritism or prejudice are blessedly reduced by the constant turnover of senior people from one post to another. The career of any individual is much less in the hands of one or two seniors than would be true in any major corporation, and certainly more so than can be seen in academic life.

Although I greatly enjoyed my 17 years in Her Majesty's Inspectorate, I was nevertheless ready for a change and welcomed the opportunity to put my name forward for the post of director of South Bank Polytechnic, as it then was. The Polytechnic was already known to me through my work, and I had great admiration for the quality of its work in engineering and the broad technological fields in which it specialized, and was particularly attracted by its proud record of service to the local population of South London. My enthusiasm was somewhat dimmed by discovering, on the first day of four days of interviews, that there were seven short-listed candidates, six of whom were men. I was inclined to give up at the end of the first day, as I thought the message about the kind of person they were looking for was written fairly clearly in the gender balance of the short-list. Fortunately, I continued through the grueling process, finding that I greatly enjoyed the opportunity provided by the format of the interviews to meet a very wide-ranging and representative cross-section of staff and students. The student union interviews were particularly stimulating because, as is so often the case, they managed to think of the most difficult questions for the candidates and refused to be impressed by any of the answers. In the democratic fashion that characterizes South Bank, the manual staff and clerical staff also had an opportunity to question the candidates; and their view, too, was fed into the final interviewing panel of the governing body.

I took up my appointment as director at the Polytechnic on 1 January 1987, the appointment having attracted considerable public and press interest because I was the first woman ever to hold such a post. Within the Polytechnic, I found little hostility on grounds of gender. The engineers and scientists preferred to get on with their work, asking only of the head of the institution that she or he provide an environment in which they could work as effectively as possible.

My almost seven years at South Bank were some of the happiest of my professional life. The excitement of that period in higher education of course needs no repetition. From 1987 to 1993, the polytechnics moved into full university status, coming out of local authority control in 1989 and attaining the university title in 1992. In the meantime, the path towards complete academic autonomy followed the route not only of freedom from local authority control but increasing freedom from the control of the Council for National Academic Awards (CNAA). This last freedom required a great deal of time, effort, and hard work on the part of those within the institutions, to ensure that the structures for academic quality control were as well-balanced as possible without the burden of unhelpful paperwork that the CNAA had increasingly imposed.

I felt greatly privileged to lead the Polytechnic into full university status in the same year that we were celebrating our centenary.

The original polytechnic, known as the Borough Polytechnic, was founded in 1892 by a distinguished group of Victorian philanthropists in a charity chaired by the Prince of Wales of that time. The first council of that South London polytechnic charity included no less than two future prime ministers. The commitment of the Victorians to technological education and to education as a vehicle for raising the living standards of the population was exemplified by the early story of the Borough Polytechnic (affectionately referred to in George Bernard Shaw's writing as the place where "all the lads had gone"). We chose the centenary year as an opportunity to raise the profile of the institution as a new university and arranged a series of events, ranging from the launch of 100 balloons from the top of the tower by Ken Horn, the television chef; through a dinner for representatives of the embassies of the European Community; an exhibition of the work of David Bomberg, who taught at the Borough Polytechnic in the 1950s; to the culmination in a service of thanksgiving in Southwark Cathedral, which provided an unforgettable opportunity to give thanks for our first founders and for the remarkable work of that dear institution over its first century.

Saying goodbye to South Bank University was a wrench, as I had so many friends there, not least among present and former students. However, other things were now occupying more and more of my time and energy; and once again it seemed right to choose to move on. In 1991 I had been given the unbelievable privilege of elevation to the Peerage by Her Majesty the Queen, with the rank of a Baron. (Although the title is Baroness, British law recognizes only Lords as members of the House of Lords, and so the official conferment for women and men alike is of a Barony of the United Kingdom.) A life peerage is a device by which an individual is turned into a legislator overnight, as a member of the upper house of parliament in this country. The House of Lords, although taking a full part in legislation, nevertheless has defined its role as a "refining and revising" chamber, in which legislation is able to be examined in more depth than is possible in the House of Commons and where there is a full understanding that the government will never be thwarted on any policy that has been part of the manifesto on which it was elected. This does not mean that on many aspects of policy the House of Lords — and not necessarily always the opposition parties — will not challenge the government where they believe that it is contrary to public interest for a particular policy to be pursued. In many quite key areas the government has accepted the arguments in the House of Lords, not least in the field of education or social policy, where there is particular expertise in the membership of the House.

Once again I found myself in a predominantly male world, as women constitute only about 5% of the membership of the House of Lords. However, the active participants in debate and legislation include a far higher proportion of women than the 5% would imply. The baronesses are by definition Life Peers, and the Life Peers constitute a high proportion of the active members of the House. Although there are about 1,000 peers who would be qualified to take part in legislative work of the House of Lords, less than 600 do so. The remainder (who include the royal family, dukes, earls of landed estates, and so on) do not pursue any legislative or political activities whatsoever.

Nevertheless, it does takes considerable courage to stand up and speak in the chamber of the House of Lords. The chamber itself is intimidatingly beautiful, and its high ceilings and plush red-leather benches were not made to encourage a feeling of informality and easy debate. The fact that every word spoken is recorded and published within hours of the end of business merely adds to the feelings of tension, even when speaking in a comparatively empty chamber. People who have been in the House for 10 or 20 years tell me this feeling of nervousness never quite disappears, and I find this encouraging. I never enter the House and climb its beautiful wide staircase, emblazoned with the arms of past military heroes ("the noble and gallant lords"), without considering myself enormously privileged and happy to be there. The quality of debate often is very high; and former cabinet ministers, former leaders of our major national and international industries, and leading members of the professions, such as judges, surgeons, vice-chancellors, and others, all bring their expertise to bear on the subject of any major debate.

Inevitably, membership of that House brings with it other responsibilities in the wider community. I have been immensely privileged to serve as a member of the prime minister's advisory panel of six on matters concerning the citizen's charter initiative. This initiative has been widely regarded around the world as a major way of encouraging all public services, including government departments, to become more oriented towards their customers than they usually have been in the past. Prime Minister John Major sees this as a way of directing the policies of all the major government departments towards the welfare of the individual citizen and empowering the individual tax payer to see her or his relationship to the public service as every bit as powerful as the relationship of any paying consumer to a commercial supplier. The challenge of carrying this through into schools and colleges is one that I find most stimulating.

I also have greatly enjoyed the challenge over the past 18 months of chairing the Department of Trade and Industry's Export Group for the Education and Training Sector. This has taken me overseas with missions to raise the profile of British education in other countries, particularly in Southeast Asia, the Middle East, and South America, and to working with British universities and colleges to encourage them to become more professional in their approach.

In July of 1994 I moved to Cambridge, which was my own beloved *alma mater*, to become president of Lucy Cavendish College. In many ways, this seems like a coming together of so many of the strands of my own career and its concerns. Lucy Cavendish is a college wholly dedicated to mature women within the University of Cambridge and so is as committed to access for women as any institution in the country. Its great challenge, however, is to find women from the mature population who are capable of achieving within this all-demanding university. The buzz and comradeship created among the remarkable women who come as our students and the equally remarkable women who form the Fellows of the college makes it a truly inspiring place in which to work. For me personally, it is an opportunity to nurture and encourage younger women into the full realization of their own potential and an opportunity to provide an example, within this university and outside, of what mature women are capable of achieving. No mission could be more important or more satisfying.

Plans for the future include making Lucy Cavendish not only a center of excellence for mature women at undergraduate and postgraduate levels but also to create here a center for women leaders from around the world, where they may enjoy periods of study, research, refreshment, and regeneration before moving forward into perhaps the highest levels in the worlds of industry, commerce, the public sector, and government.

I know myself to be an immensely fortunate person. I once had a note from a very dear lady in her eighties, who summed up her life by saying she had been immensely blessed to have enjoyed children, grandchildren, and a life of public service. She ended with the Latin words *laeta sors mea* — "happy is my lot." I echo her thought. I, too, find my lot to be a very happy one. I have 43 years of a wonderful marriage and a most beloved husband; I have four very dear children, now pursuing their own lives but remaining with each other and with us as a family united in love; I have, so far, four adorable grandchildren; and I have a professional life that has brought friendships, learning, and growth beyond my wildest dream. I now look forward, in this next stage of my life in Cambridge, to passing on some of the learning and growth I have enjoyed to the younger generation of women around me.

Gillian L. Slater

OH, POOR YOU!
by Gillian L. Slater

Gillian L. Slater is vice-chancellor of Bournemouth University. After attending Sutton High School for Girls, she earned B.A., M.Sc., and D. Phil. degrees in mathematics from the University of Oxford. She taught mathematics and some aspects of computer science at South Bank and Sheffield City Polytechnics (now universities) before assuming the post of head of the Department of Mathematics and Physics, and later dean of Science and Engineering and professor at Manchester Polytechnic (now also a university).

After two years as pro-vice-chancellor at Manchester Metropolitan University, Professor Slater was appointed vice-chancellor of Bournemouth University in 1994. Her research interests, publications, and consultancies are in the areas of mathematical modeling, system design, and formal methods of software engineering. Her current interests are in mechanisms of technology transfer and university-industry relationships. Professor Slater's community involvement includes service previously as a director of the Trafford Park Manufacturing Institute and currently as a director of Dorset Chamber of Commerce and Industry and of Business Link Dorset, Ltd.

There has been only one significant occasion in my life when I was forced to feel disadvantaged by my gender. I found myself facing an interview panel across the board room of a football club from England's premier league. As an academic and a mother of daughters, I had not been in a football ground, even less the club buildings, since my teenage years. English football clubs remain very much a male preserve. The circumstances were not a career-change decision; I was being interviewed for the post of vice-chancellor of one of the United Kingdom's large universities. Regrettably, the chairman of the university board also was chairman of the board of the football club and had decided to interview at the ground rather than at the university. Uncomfortable, I

201

responded badly, and the interview was a disaster from the first minute — with the inevitable consequences. I did not complain — "nice" women do not do that sort of thing — but the incident made me far more aware of unintentional discrimination.

I am a believer in the hand of fate. That job would not have been right for me. Since December 1994, I have held the post of vice-chancellor of Bournemouth University — the most enjoyable job I have ever done. Bournemouth is a new university. In 1976 Bournemouth College of Technology and Weymouth College of Education merged to form Dorset Institute of Higher Education. After 14 years of rapid change and growth, it gained polytechnic status in 1990 and university status in 1992, with student numbers rising from 2,600 FTE (full-time equivalents) in 1982 to 8,500 FTE in 1994. The university serves the conurbation of Poole, Bournemouth, and Christchurch, which has a population of 400,000. It has partner colleges in Bournemouth, Poole, the Isle of Wight, and Yeovil in Somerset and has strong European connections.

Bournemouth is a pleasant town on the south coast of England. Regarded by many as a holiday center, it currently is working on developing its tourist image to capture new markets. The university is strongly vocational and has 49 first-degree and 31 postgraduate courses, in addition to a range of professional and short courses. There currently are about 1,000 postgraduate students. The university has introduced a number of highly innovative courses and has a good success rate in placing students in work.

The role of the vice-chancellor is to be the academic leader; to represent the university locally, nationally, and internationally; to improve the funding income, particularly from research and consultancy; and to oversee control of the budget. The office of the vice-chancellor includes a deputy vice-chancellor, a pro vice-chancellor (academic), and a director of human resources. The senior management team consists of seven heads of school and eight heads of support services. The vice-chancellor is a member of the university board, the chief executive of the university, and chairman of the university senate, which is the main academic policy group.

Carrying out these duties, of course, covers an amazing variety of activities, from making short speeches of welcome at conferences, including on one occasion responding to a speech in Latin, to ensuring that the strategic plan for the university is realistic and does indeed reflect the future of the university as we wish it to be; from talking to local politicians to dealing with the Higher Education Funding Council. As I write, I have been in post for less than a year, and so my impressions are very much still first impressions.

Although my post has the responsibility for the overall academic leadership of the university, I also am the chief executive and carry financial and administrative responsibilities. To assist me in these roles, I have undertaken various development activities in the area of management and especially university management. I believe in using information technology as support, and there is a laptop computer on my desk, which I use. My aim is to employ the tools of management to the best advantage whilst setting all in an academic environment.

I am helped in my role by the university chancellor, Baroness Cox of Queensbury. Lady Cox has numerous activities, many of them undertaken in remote parts of the world, and yet she finds time to visit the university regularly and always is interested in our activities. We believe that Bournemouth is the only British university with women as both chancellor and vice-chancellor.

My training demands a sense of order in this essay, and so I will "begin at the beginning and carry on until I reach the end and then stop" to paraphrase Alice's instructions. I was born in 1949 in South London to a middle-class family, the only daughter of a company accountant and a housewife, with no family background of higher education. My father was a very clever man whose parents could not have afforded higher education. From my mother I acquired a level of innate common sense and practicality without which I would not now hold my position. Education being "important for boys," my younger brother attended a private nursery, a prep school, and then one of the better public schools. I went to the state infants and junior school and then won a place at the local girls' grammar school. The grammar school was excellent, and at that time I saw nothing strange that my parents were scrimping to pay for my brother's education but not for mine. However, it has affected my attitude to the education I have tried to secure for my daughters.

In my last year at school, I succeeded in obtaining a place at Oxford University to read mathematics and a scholarship from IBM to pay all my costs of so doing. I enjoyed Oxford immensely and made many long-lasting friendships there. I also became active in student politics — this was the late 1960s, a time of student revolt — as well as party politics. My one regret is that I never spoke at the Oxford Union, though I attended many debates. A love of subject and an enjoyment of internal politics seem often to be the hallmark of an academic.

I became a research student at Oxford and worked in the field of functional differential equations. During this period I married a fellow research student, completed my M.Sc. and D.Phil. in three years, and made two discoveries that had a profound effect on my future. To help make ends meet, like most research students, I gave tutorials in my specialist field for undergraduates at several colleges and assisted with first year examples classes. I discovered that I thoroughly enjoyed teaching. My research problem had arisen from one of the Oxford Study Groups with Industry and involved investigating the solution set of an equation which arose in the modeling of the overhead power supply to a train — mathematics could really be useful and was so much more than the private game it so often had appeared to be. Securing a lecturing post in London at the Polytechnic of the South Bank — now South Bank University — was a clear statement of these two attributes. I wanted to teach in higher education, and I wanted to teach in a vocational environment. The polytechnics were newly formed then — the brain child of Anthony Crosland.

As a young lecturer, I did not meet my head of department often; but the calm, collected, and friendly management style of John Dubbey as head of Mathematics and Computing at South Bank Polytechnic has remained an influence, though I have not met him again for 15 years. Being friendly but not "one of the gang" is the balance that every leader strives to achieve. Many are so concerned at protecting their dignity that they remain cold and aloof, which is even less productive than the leader who is indistinguishable from his team. A stable equilibrium is most inclined to lead to outstanding success, and it probably is the achievement of this balance that causes me to question my own activities more than other issues of management.

A fairly standard university lecturing career then followed, with promotion and relocation eventually to a senior lectureship at Sheffield City Polytechnic (now Sheffield Hallam University). I had always undertaken a substantial teaching load (24 hours of class contact per week at one stage in the early days) and was probably happiest in the lecture theater or seminar room; but I had remained reasonably active in research, changing fields to the applications of mathematics in computer science. At this point I was offered a change of emphasis. Would I lead a fully funded project to develop a video learning pack for industry to be written by a large, diverse, and scattered project team? It would mean a year without any teaching, with really no time for any research; but it would be doing something interesting, worthwhile, and different for me. I accepted and found myself managing and leading a team for the first time. It was hectic, frustrating, infuriating, and thoroughly rewarding. We delivered the pack on time and within budget, and I had thoroughly enjoyed persuading others to do what I wanted. Fortunately, I was able to exercise these powers further almost immediately by my appointment to the post of head of Mathematics and Physics at Manchester Polytechnic (now Manchester Metropolitan University).

I was used to working in a world that was predominantly male, and I enjoyed that atmosphere. Previously there had always been a couple of other women lecturers in the departments in which I had worked, so that a chat about family as well as sport was occasionally possible. Manchester was different. All the departmental academic and technical staff were men. All the other heads of department in the faculty were men. It did feel rather lonely, especially as I also was trying to raise two children on my own at that stage — fortunately not for long. There was plenty to be done, and I started to make course and organizational changes and to raise the level of research activity in the department. The staff worked well as a team, and the results were far better than my expectations and achieved without too much of the infighting that can be a feature of academic departments.

Settled and leading a department that was achieving well, I was not thinking of any change of career. Teaching was still my first love, but I was enjoying the management and administrative tasks. Research had been reduced to writing a book with a colleague who essentially did all of the work. There had been an opportunity to apply for the post of assistant director and dean of the faculty, and it really had not occurred to me to consider this. One of my colleagues, Alan Sweetman, had far better experience than mine for the job. My children were 11 and 7, so I did not really want any more responsibility. Alan was appointed to the post, and two terms later, in the middle of many major new initiatives, he suffered a heart attack on the last day of the spring term and died at the age of 46. To this day, I try to remember Alan whenever I feel myself beginning to feel stressed. He has become a talisman to force me to take a deep breath and to reduce the anxiety level.

I was asked to take over in an acting capacity and later appointed to the post after competitive interview. It was an excellent time to make the sort of changes that could lead to real progress. I took over as the polytechnic came away from local authority control and became a self-governing institution answerable to its board of governors and to the Polytechnic and Colleges Funding Council, a buffer organization between institutions and national government. Internally, after a batch of early retirements, I had the chance to appoint heads to many of the departments in the faculty. During my five years in this post, the polytechnics achieved university status; and we became Manchester Metropolitan University and I became a pro-vice-chancellor.

During this time I was helped by the support and friendship of Doug Hamer, then deputy director of the Polytechnic. Although not someone to hesitate in pointing out your sins, Doug is a friend who always has time for others and is always ready to offer his advice — not that I always took it, but that did not trouble him either.

I also learned much throughout this period from Sir Kenneth Green, the vice-chancellor of Manchester Metropolitan University. The opportunity to work directly for one of the major players on the national higher education stage was exceptional, and there is much to admire in Sir Kenneth. I learned most clearly at this stage that there is at least one other side to every story and that it is advisable to hear all the evidence before acting. There are many ways in which to chair a meeting; the style to chose depends on the results you wish to achieve. Sir Kenneth was very supportive in my career development and was keen for me to move on to the right next post. As a result of this, I found myself in the football club mentioned earlier and now in post at Bournemouth. I have, on occasion, summed up my time at Manchester Met with a remark that, while trite, is also apt and characterizes my working relationship with Sir Kenneth, who is of great height. "It's not easy to see eye to eye with someone who is six feet seven inches tall, but it's always worth trying."

My life is made more complicated but immeasurably more pleasurable by my two daughters, currently aged 18 and 14. It was the opening of a workplace nursery at South Bank in 1977 that showed me that a career and children might both be possible. This is accepted practice now; but at the time, I was regarded as slightly unusual. The stories of their early years are the cocktail of crises, pride, and exhaustion that every working mother knows. The choices between attending a professional meeting or a parent-teacher evening, between an examination board and the school Christmas play are still having to be made, but now I know that there is never a right answer. My daughters are the better for the independence they have been forced to develop; and because they (usually) appreciate my dilemma, there is a strong bond between us.

This essay is titled "Oh, Poor You!" and I have left its explanation to the end. Early in my career when I was introduced to the vice-chancellor of one of England's established universities, he asked about my work. I explained that I lectured at a polytechnic. He responded, "Oh, poor you." It was not appropriate at the time and, using this article as an opportunity to review my career, it is far from appropriate now.

Janet Trotter

THE NATURE OF JOURNEYING
by Janet Trotter

Janet Trotter is director of Cheltenham and Gloucester College of Higher Education. She attended the Secondary Technical School for Girls in Maidstone before earning Certificates with Honors in Education and Religious Teaching from Bishop Lonsdale College of Education followed by an Academic Diploma in Theology, a Bachelor of Divinity degree, and a Master of Arts in Education and Theology from the University of London (external programs). Her final degree, also earned through part-time study, was a Master of Science in Business Administration from the University of Brunel and Henley Administrative College. After teaching in secondary schools and at King Alfred's College, Winchester, she became head of professional studies at that institution and then served a secondment to Church House, Westminster, taking responsibility for the 11 surviving Church Colleges while they became part of the British national funding system for higher education.

In 1990, Ms. Trotter became director of Cheltenham and Gloucester College of Higher Education, a merger of the College of St. Paul and St. Mary (where she had served as principal since 1986) and the Higher Education Courses of the Gloucestershire College of Arts and Technology. Her services to education were honored by Queen Elizabeth in 1991 with the Order of the British Empire.

There is about every journey a sense of anticipation and expectation. Such questions as "What will I see?" and "Who will I meet?" dominate the mind in addition to the routine ones about whether essential items of equipment have been packed. I have a strong sense of life as a journey with a dynamic that calls me both onwards and inwards — onwards in the sense that I have a restlessness to contribute to the corporate journey that humanity shares and inwards in that the external is mirrored by a journey to greater self-understanding and realization.

Equipment of the Journey

Before embarking on any journey, there are preparations to make and bags to pack. What does one pack for a professional journey? What, amongst the vast array of possible qualities and possessions, should be acquired as key elements of equipment? Three items of "equipment" have been precious accompaniments on my journey — family, education, and faith — and they have been valuable resources in times of difficulty and at moments of achievement.

I was born into a loving family that continues to love and support me. It was difficult being a child in the last years of the second war in Europe and in the immediate postwar period. The small family unit (my mother, sister, and me) was close while my father was away in an active service unit in Europe. I can remember well the darkness and shadows of Chatham, a dockyard town; the wrecks of men returning from war; the homesickness as I went to nursery school; the long walks in the countryside; my first bicycle; holidays at my grandmother's in Hampshire; flying kites and making music — in all respects, ordinary experiences for a child growing up in the 1940s and 1950s.

My mother was always there, willing to listen and talk things through. In a sense she has been, and continues to be, a powerful role model. Before the war she moved from kitchen maid to chief cook in a series of large houses, and in times of plenty and in times of scarcity she has always shown inventiveness and resourcefulness in the kitchen. She is a model of selfless offering in that she has seen her own fulfillment in launching the family into the world.

My father left school at 14 and became a clerk and then a garage mechanic. In 1938 he entered the police force and painstakingly pursued a correspondence course, passing his examinations and becoming the youngest sergeant in the Kent force. His deep understanding of everything mechanical enabled him to become a key member of the traffic force, teaching at the driving school and rising to the position of superintendent. My father was, and still is, a strict disciplinarian; but I appreciate his integrity and honesty. He has a clarity of mind and a rootedness in both time and place.

My formal education was not atypical. I failed to gain entrance to a grammar school at 11 and, having had two happy years at a secondary modern, moved at 13 to a technical school. By that time I was beginning to take an active interest in reading, literature, the arts, and music; and I thrived on the regimentation of this all-girls school. The daily routine gave me an opportunity to think, and I was fortunate to have some dedicated teachers to stimulate that thought. At 16 my parents were committed to my leaving school — they both believed that I could succeed without further education — but I managed to persuade them that a career in teaching was a viable option. And so I was allowed to remain at school until I had achieved my higher education entrance qualifications at the age of 17.

It was then, at my father's instigation, that I worked as a nursing orderly in a hospital for a year prior to going to college. During that year I matured immeasurably and came to appreciate the agony of watching families suffering with loved ones during terminal illness and the value of education in a democratic society. Thus equipped with missionary zeal for education, I headed for college in Derby to train to teach religious education. It was an interesting phase: knowing financial hardship, being tested to the core in the classroom with difficult inner-city children, but enjoying the experience of study and reflection.

During my early teenage years I developed a commitment to religion and to the spiritual quest. Possibly because of my memories of the postwar period, I had become obsessed by the Jewish question and by the complex reasons for the Holocaust. How could a generation have been persuaded to pursue a policy of genocide by such a leader, and how could the Jews of Europe have made sense of such an experience without faith? Exploring such questions made me want to do my bit to make the world more livable for future generations. My years at college confirmed my love of biblical study and my interest in multi-faith and multicultural issues, both enduring themes and touchstones in my life.

On leaving Derby, I had a restless urge to achieve a degree and immediately registered for an external academic diploma in theology at London University and, when successful, embarked on a Bachelor of Divinity program. I achieved this in 1974 after five years of correspondence courses, private New Testament Greek lessons, and long hours of study. This aptitude for part-time study has remained with me, and in 1978 I gained a master's degree in education and theology and in 1984 an M.Sc. in business administration.

My motivation to undertake this study has been a wish to be more effective at the job I do rather than to prepare for the next job. It also has toughened me up, so that now I am able to concentrate for formidably long hours and to stay with a project to its completion.

Key Staging Posts on My Professional Journey

Between 1965 and 1974 I taught in three secondary schools in Kent. Despite a certain nervousness about the privilege and responsibility involved in teaching, I loved it more than I had imagined possible. I spent long hours preparing lessons and trying to make complex material accessible — and fun.

It often is said that the successful teacher is an exhibitionist and good "performer." On the contrary, experience led to the belief that the most successful teaching occurs when one is not "performing" but encountering other human beings, with all strengths and weaknesses, and exploring ideas and concepts together.

All of the head teachers for whom I worked took an interest in my development and encouraged me to experiment. I introduced revised syllabi in religious education, adopted new approaches to morning assembly, and developed community service programs. Each innovation was carefully researched and thoroughly planned; and as I succeeded, I grew in confidence.

In 1973-74, at the age of 29, I was being recommended for deputy headships; and I reflected for some time on my suitability for such a role. I was comparatively inexperienced, enjoyed teaching, and wanted to contribute to the broader educational picture. I decided, therefore, to seek a lecturer post in a college of education, believing that if I was successful, I would return to school management at a later date. I was appointed to a lectureship in Education and Religious Studies at King Alfred's College, Winchester, in 1974 and stayed there, in a variety of roles, for almost 12 years. I was recruited in a sizable group of other young lecturers, and we bonded into an energetic and creative force.

While at King Alfred's I took the conscious decision not to pursue research in theology. I preferred to devote time to action-research related to curriculum development. I became involved in a number of research projects and particularly valued membership on the creative team that led to a series of publications, including the influential *Paths to Understanding*, which revolutionized religious education in Hampshire schools.

My most significant role at the college was as head of professional studies, which involved managing and developing the curriculum of 1,000 or so teacher-training students with a staff of about 40. I greatly enjoyed the supervision of students in school and increasingly came to appreciate my visits to First Schools, where I became fascinated by the mysterious minds of those children in their first stages of learning. In many ways, I still regard my period as head of professional studies as the most creative in my career. Middle management can afford scope for rapid change that it is sometimes difficult to achieve as an organizational head. I was responsible for taking the college into a partnership of four church colleges in the east end of London — the Urban Learning Foundation. This provided opportunities for our very best teacher education students to have inner-city, multicultural classroom experience prior to qualification; and it is gratifying that this kindled in many a commitment to work in such settings. I also was instrumental in launching innovative partnership links with schools.

It was while undertaking this role that I acquired strategic planning skills and the ability to switch from big-picture issues to the seeming minutia of day-to-day management.

Development, in my experience, always is accompanied by some pain; and King Alfred's brought its fair share. I learned hard lessons about myself from encounter groups, which were much the vogue then, both in the church and at college. I also faced petty jealousies, male-dominated management styles, and the pleasure and pain of department management, which I believe to be the most demanding role in an academic environment.

In the summer of 1985 I was scheduled to have a sabbatical to complete my M.Sc.; but a week before it was scheduled to begin, I was invited to undertake a six-month secondment to Church House, Westminster, to be responsible for the 11 surviving church colleges. Despite the pressures of study, I decided to accept the secondment, and I enjoyed watching summer change to autumn from my garret above Westminster Abbey. This was a significant period for the church colleges, as they became part of the national funding system for higher education rather than subject to a different funding regime directly related to the Department of Education and Science. In this role I developed an interest in national higher education politics and, helpfully, met a large number of people who were significant on the national stage. I also learned that, for me, a collegiate setting is preferred to that of a civil-servant role because of my interest in working closely with both staff and students in a learning organization.

Following a short interlude back at King Alfred's, I moved to St. Martin's College, Lancaster, as vice principal in 1985. The principal, Robert Clayton, was a gifted leader and always put students at the center of college life. From our offices overlooking the expanse of Morecambe Bay with its ever-changing landscape, we worked in a companionable relationship until a telephone call in November from the chairman of governors at the College of St. Paul and St. Mary, Cheltenham, led to an invitation to become principal there. I left Lancaster with many regrets, not least the sense that the head-hunting process had propelled me into moving at a pace dictated by the external environment rather than by my own internal promptings.

The College of St. Paul and St. Mary (CPM) was founded in 1847 by a group of evangelical church people, and the majority of its work was devoted to teacher training. Like many other colleges during the 1980s, it was fairly static and sleepy when I arrived in 1986. It was clear to me, given that the United Kingdom was in the midst of the Thatcher years, that the college had to change in fundamental ways if it was to survive to the 21st century. The opportunity came for this when the Education Reform Act was published in 1987, and a merger between CPM and the higher education courses of the Gloucestershire College of Arts and Technology (GLOSCAT) was mooted. Many forces at that time encouraged me to "take over" the GLOSCAT courses, but I was repelled by the notion of "taking over" academics and set my sights on achieving a stable and viable institution by creating a new organization. The merger was complex, as GLOSCAT needed to demerge before merging with CPM. Changes in culture and approach also pervaded the two merging partners. But the decision to develop a modular curriculum was astute, as it provided an academic market place in which colleagues could re-ally and regroup.

The new college, the Cheltenham and Gloucester College of Higher Education (CGCHE), was born in April 1990 with 3,000 full-time higher education students. Now, four years later and following a stimulation of the higher education market, we have 5,500 full-time students and a range of part-time programs. We also offer our own degrees up to master's level by agreement with the Privy Council and feel that the infant college is growing to maturity.

Nevertheless, the new college has had its fair share of birth pangs, including financial problems, a lack of the appropriate management skills in the right places, and a publicly controversial estates strategy.

There is no doubt that I find being a public figure one of the most difficult aspects of my current job, particularly when criticism is founded on misinformation. Throughout difficulties, the talent and potential of staff, students, and the new institution itself have made it bearable. In fact, I continue to find the challenges great fun.

During this period I have had a number of publicly appointed roles that have been, in a strange way, therapeutic because they keep me from becoming obsessed by the college's birth pangs. In the first of these, I act as chair of Gloucestershire Health Authority, the purchasing arm of the National Health Service provision in the county. This organization, which has a budget of £280 million to purchase health care for 540,000 people, has an involvement in medical technology, user and care groups, quality care, public consultation, medical ethics, and public policy. The enormity of the role is daunting, but the insights I gain from involvement in another public service that is undergoing reform are fascinating and revealing. The executive and non-executive colleagues whom I meet also have provided friendship and new perspectives on managing a complex organization.

I also am a member of the Higher Education Funding Council, which funds, on behalf of government, all higher education in England; and I now look forward to joining the Teacher Training Agency this autumn.

It was a delight to be honored by the Queen in 1991, for services to education, with the Order of the British Empire.

Companions on the Journey

I have been fortunate to have traveled with three significant and gifted companions. Each has brought a unique contribution to my journey. They have been with me as I have traversed difficult terrain, helping to re-establish the pathway. At other times they have celebrated the achievements associated with crossing turbulent rivers in full spate.

I first met *A* during a conference on multi-faith/plural education in Birmingham in the early 1970s. He was the chair of the conference, and I was immediately impressed by his typically Jewish wit and wisdom. During conversations I discovered that he was a rabbi of the reformed synagogue movement, that he had been a child in Auschwitz, and that his life had been devoted to building up the shattered Jewish community following the Sec-

218

ond World War. At the end of the conference he invited me to join him for lunch in London during a visit, but I did nothing to take up this offer until, in his typical fashion, he sent me a Christmas card saying the invitation was still open. Since that time I have seen him for lunch on a regular basis. I am aware that at times the conversation is dominated by my agenda and other times by his — whoever speaks or whoever listens, we talk in a way that encourages total honesty. Whether it is on the state of Israel, a management problem, or the Thatcher years in the United Kingdom, he has the capacity to peel away the layers of the worldly onion skin to expose the world and myself as they are. There is a deepness and honesty in the relationship that is rare, and through difficult times I have been supported by this most trustworthy of companions.

My second companion is *B*, whom I first met in the mid-1970s. At that time he was a personnel manager at ICI, the chemical company. He also was an active member of the United Kingdom committee of St. George's College Jerusalem, a college of which I was governor and at which I lectured most summers during the 1970s and early 1980s. Over a business dinner one evening in 1978, I discussed with him my management responsibilities at college and my sense of unease at having no formal management training. He advised me to take a course or a secondment to industry, and the following year I enrolled for a part-time M.Sc. in business administration at the Henley Management College. As I hesitantly confronted, for me, the mystical world of double-entry bookkeeping and management science, he was there to help me with percentages and management accounts.

B is the son of a Grimsby fisherman, but in the Thirties made his way to Oxford to take a degree in geography. Now, in his seventies, after a career in the Colonial Service, in ICI, and in the Middle East Association, he is spending his retirement pursuing a Ph.D., the research for which entails exploring the pattern of Muslim settlement in the city of Birmingham. He has a number of invaluable qualities in a traveling companion. He has an insatiable curiosity and is painstaking in getting to the heart of a mat-

219

ter. He always is urging me to research a problem thoroughly; and when I am too goal-oriented, he encourages me to turn aside from the straight path and admire the view. If ever I have the need to talk something over or explore a range of options, I have been able to rely on his intellectual capacities. As with *A*, *B* is not first and foremost admired for his mind but for his selflessness, which springs from his religious commitment, a commitment that is not narrow and rigid but open to the in-dwelling of the holy spirit in people of different races, colors, and creeds.

My third companion, and a late comer to the journey, is a very different companion. Soon after I accepted the principalship at Cheltenham I realized that solving the inherent problems of the building stock would remain with me for my professional life in the town. Now, eight years on and after public inquiries, death threats, media abuse, and achievements as well as setbacks, I recognize the importance of *C*, a quantity surveyor and the buildings project manager. He is a Yorkshireman who left school at 16 and trained to become a quantity surveyor. He was recommended to the college in 1989 and was engaged to develop a college building strategy and implement it. Through his skill I have come to appreciate the built environment, the complexity of modern buildings, and the value of buildings fit for their purpose in the development of a modern college. I admire his management style, which stresses the value of gathering a quality team for a project, researching solutions, and tough negotiation.

Reflections on the Journey Thus Far

One of my favorite pieces of writing is a poem by the Welsh poet R.S. Thomas, titled "Pilgrimage." It describes a group of pilgrims journeying up a cobbled path to a church on an isolated island off the coast of Wales. When they arrive they expect somehow to find God within this ancient holy place. Instead, Thomas comments that the sense of having arrived is erroneous for, "He is such a fast God. Always before us and leaving as we arrive."

My personal journey is associated with such a God, and I reach 50 years of age with a sense of more to do and more to learn.

My story to date indicates that I value particularly my family's support and my faith, education, and traveling companions — nothing, in a sense, extraordinary. But what have I learned so far?

With regard to management style, I am constantly trying to obtain a higher grade on my own marking scale. Managing the Cheltenham and Gloucester College is complex, and there always is opportunity for improvement. I try to be firm, fair, honest, well-prepared, and supportive.

Given the trebling in student numbers in the past five years, I have had to adjust to delegating and relying on others, rather than doing everything myself; and I have found this difficult. I still feel guilty when staff say that they see less of me. But management by walking away can be equally as important for empowerment as management by walking about, and reaching the right balance is an important skill.

One of the principals for whom I worked previously commented that one of the qualities in me that he had appreciated was "steadiness." I can remember that I felt perplexed by this expression — I would like to have been considered hardworking, creative, and dynamic. I now know, however, that this quality is one that I prize in others. For me it is not charisma that keeps organizations well-oiled, successful, and responsive, but steadiness that is manifested in clear goals, effective teamwork, and a commitment to developing individual potential.

Dorothy Wedderburn

A LIFETIME OF LEARNING

by Dorothy Wedderburn

Dorothy Wedderburn was the founding principal of Royal Holloway and Bedford New College, University of London. After attending Walthamstow High School for Girls, she earned B.A. and M.A. degrees in economics from Girton College, Cambridge University. She served as a senior research officer at Cambridge in the Department of Applied Economics, professor of industrial sociology and head of the Department of Economics and Social Studies at Imperial College, and visiting professor at the Sloan School of Management at the Massachusetts Institute of Technology.

Professor Wedderburn was principal of Bedford College, University of London, from 1981 until its merger with Royal Holloway to form the new college. She has been a member of various government bodies, including the Royal Commission on the Distribution of Income and Wealth and the Council of the Advisory Conciliation and Arbitration Service. She currently is senior research fellow in the Management School, Imperial College of Science, Technology, and Medicine. Professor Wedderburn has been awarded honorary doctorates from the Universities of Warwick, Loughborough, Brunel, City, and Cambridge. Her research, books, and articles address sociology, economics, management, and higher education policy.

Two years ago I attended a reunion of those of us who had gone up to Girton College, Cambridge, in October 1943 as "freshers." As we exchanged news about ourselves, I was struck by how much the experiences of women graduates have changed. Very few of my generation had followed "careers." Most had entered the teaching profession for a few years; most had married quite soon, had children, and had given up regular work until their middle age. Yet those women were clever; they were highly selected. There were only 50,000 university undergraduates in the country just before the Second World War; the number of women among them was minuscule, and access to Oxford and Cambridge was very competitive. But it is clear that even clever young women graduates did not expect to have careers in the 1940s and 1950s. I was no exception. The story of how I came to follow the career I did, first as a university professor and then, for ten years before my retirement at 65, as the first woman head of a mixed-sex higher education institution, is at one level the story of the broadening of education access to include both more people of working and lower-middle-class origin and, also, of women. At another level, it is a story of my personal response to these changing opportunities.

I was myself of working-class origin. My father was a craftsman, a joiner and cabinet maker. My mother was born in rural Norfolk, left school at 13, and entered domestic service first locally and then in London in the household of a Church of England clergyman. She married my father at the age of 28 just before the First World War. I was the last of three children, born as a substitute for the oldest girl who at the age of 13 had died of rheumatic fever. The second child, my brother, became an important influence in my life. He was very clever and won a scholarship to Cambridge to read mathematics, followed by research at Princeton. After a significant contribution in the Second World War as a statistician, he became an academic with an international reputation. It was he who supported me when I showed signs of wanting to go to university.

In our family it was my father, not my mother, who was the parent who valued education, not least because he never forgot that the poverty of his own family had denied him an opportunity to go to grammar school. I well remember that when I was sitting entrance examinations for Oxford or Cambridge, my mother asked, "What is the use of her going to college? She will only get married." My father's response was terse, "Her brother had the opportunity — so should she," and this was despite the fact that it would delay the possibility of my making a much-needed financial contribution to the household income.

Before the Second World War, access to grammar school education was selective. Having passed the examination, I entered an all-girls school in East London. After three happy years, war broke out and we were all evacuated to the Midlands. Looking back now, I am astounded at how we managed to acquire a decent education. We were sent to live with families of diverse origins. I lived with a Dutch family, which contrasted greatly with my own family circumstances. Lessons in the morning were delivered in the run-down home of the local YMCA. School buildings with laboratories and library were available only in the afternoon. Our teachers (all unmarried) became very close to us, though I cannot say that any one of them became a role model for me. We returned to London just as we embarked on our entrance examinations for university. Two of us from my year were successful. (Our names are still there on the Honours Board in the London school.) I had been offered places at both Oxford and Cambridge but chose the latter largely because that was my brother's university, and his wife had actually been a student at Girton, which was to become my college.

Cambridge was a confusing experience. From the point of view of women, it was hostile. We were clearly segregated as far as the colleges were concerned. In 1943 there were only two colleges that admitted women and all the fellowship of those two was female. I was reading economics. Lectures were provided on a university-wide basis. In other subjects there were a few women lecturers, but there was only one woman in the economics faculty (although the fact that she was Joan Robinson made up for a lot). On the other hand, from 1943-45 male undergraduates were thin on the ground because so many were doing war service. It was thus easier for women to attain positions of prominence in university societies. However, on reflection, I do not think it was my femaleness that made me feel an outsider. Rather, it was my class background. There was only a handful of other working-class (or even lower-middle-class) girls at Girton, and we found the articulateness and apparent self-assurance of our fellows, from Roedean and Cheltenham Ladies College, quite overwhelming. Another factor that contributed to the sense of not "belonging"

225

was my membership in the Communist Party, which I joined as soon as I arrived in Cambridge.

In retrospect I see that the party provided a remarkable training for women. Among intellectuals, and in the atmosphere of war time, I was not aware of any gender discrimination. It was important to be a good student; and in order to win support for party policy, members were encouraged to be active in other student bodies, to participate in political debates and discussions, and to provide efficient organizational skills. Thus I soon became "noticeable" among my contemporaries. At the same time Communists were always a minority group and were always regarded with some suspicion, which of course grew after 1945 when the "Cold War" developed. At the end of three years when I graduated, these conflicting influences and experiences left me with much self-doubt. Of course, I knew I had done well to get to Cambridge and to win the scholarships I needed to pay my way. Yet I had got "only" an upper-second-class degree and I retained a sneaking feeling that it was all a mistake and at some point I would be "found out."

Graduation in 1946 also found me with no clear idea of what I wanted to do. An academic career never crossed my mind. I cared deeply about finding a socially useful niche, and a Labour Government had just been elected in an almost euphoric atmosphere. There was a widespread desire never to return to the prewar evils of poverty and unemployment but to lay the foundation of a more socially just society. I decided, therefore, that it would be good to become part of government and to join the civil service in a division of the Board of Trade. At this time I married a contemporary from Cambridge, who was still serving in the Royal Air Force. Two years later he was demobilized and naturally returned to Cambridge to finish his degree. Just as naturally, I assumed I would go with him and eventually found that I could transfer to the Board of Trade regional office in Cambridge but in a research role, rather than an administrative role. I enjoyed this work. I also renewed contacts with Cambridge economists and was soon approached about taking a job in a newly established applied economics research institute in the economics faculty. I jumped at the chance. At the same time, I began to teach undergraduates, part time, on the one-to-one system of supervision for which Oxbridge has become famous. Although I was scarcely aware of it, my career as an academic had started.

Over the next two or three years my aspirations crystallized. I decided I wished to become a full university lecturer, but it never occurred to me to apply for posts that would take me away from my husband. Apart from any other considerations, I assumed that I would have children and, when I did, I would give up working, at least for a time. And so I remained as a research officer, though I was slowly promoted through the research hierarchy; and it was here that I encountered my first and only overt example of discrimination. A senior slot in the department was to be filled. There were two strong candidates, of whom I was one. We both had good publication records and were both initiating research programs. But the appointments committee was swayed by the argument that I was married to a Cambridge don and would therefore be most unlikely to move away to take another job. When I heard this, my indignation was great and my protests made the committee reconsider their decision in my favor, and so I became a senior research officer. But those who had argued that I would be tied to my husband were right in their judgment, for in 1965, when he had accepted a chair in London University, I moved to a full lectureship at Imperial College of Science and Technology.

Throughout this period, even after leaving the Communist Party, I remained politically engaged with the "left." Disillusionment with the Soviet Union had not (and still has not) weakened my belief that it is possible to combine greater democracy with greater social justice and harmony. I joined the Labour Party. In the 1960s most of my energies were devoted to the peace movement and, in particular, to the Campaign for Nuclear Disarmament, then at the peak of its influence. The need to engage with the scientific arguments around nuclear weaponry revived my interest in the way in which science policy was structured and developed in the Cold War world. Moreover, the gulf between the "two cultures," as described by C.P. Snow, had always fascinated me. Thus the offer of a post at Imperial College, an institution almost exclusively concerned with teaching and research in the engineering and science disciplines, was intriguing. A few influential members among the senior academic staff had formed the view that Imperial students would benefit from a better understanding of the economic and social context, at both macro- and micro-level, in which they would be applying their knowledge. They had succeeded in persuading the college that a lectureship in economics and industrial sociology should be created, and it was to this lectureship that I came in 1965.

In addition, there were other attractions for me at Imperial. My research interests at Cambridge initially had focused on the economics of social policy, generally and particularly on problems of aging, poverty, and inequality. But studies of unemployment and the process of redundancy had encouraged an interest in industrial organization. A year at the London School of Economics to study sociology, then not a subject recognized at Cambridge, had convinced me that the subject of economics, increasingly dominated by mathematical approaches, was moving farther and farther away from the "real world." I came to regard myself as an industrial sociologist. I embarked on a major study of the way in which the technology of production systems influenced both management structures and workers' attitudes and behavior. I had discovered that Joan Woodward, then a reader in industrial sociology in the management science group at Imperial, was herself working in this area, and the idea of collaborating with her excited me.

In retrospect, I understand how once again I had positioned myself as something of an outsider on two counts. The first was sex. When Joan Woodward was appointed to the chair of Industrial Sociology at Imperial College in 1970, she was only the second woman professor in the history of the institution. As for women undergraduates, there were only a handful. (The washrooms were labeled "staff," "students," and "women.") The second count was in respect of my academic discipline. Although there were visionaries among the scientists and engineers who supported the activities of what became the Industrial Sociology Unit, there also was much hostility. Thus, in addition to our teaching and research, we were forced to assume the role of missionaries within the college, constantly fighting for a position, building a public presence, and seeking opportunities to explain what we were about.

About this time, my external public commitments began to multiply and my national and, indeed, international reputation was growing. Many visits were made to the United States to lecture and present papers on various aspects of social policy. I became a consultant to the Manpower and Social Affairs Directorate of the Organisation for Economic Cooperation and Development, and the work I was doing on technology and management organization led to involvement with major industrial companies, including ICI and International Harvester. These varied experiences were immensely valuable in introducing me to relationships in the non-academic world and providing an understanding of the processes involved in the negotiation of consensus between groups with differing backgrounds and objectives.

Sadly, in 1971 Joan Woodward died of cancer at the early age of 55. The period between her death and my own appointment to a chair in 1975 was not an easy one. Those in Imperial College who always had doubted the wisdom of supporting alien activities in the social sciences seized the opportunity to insist on a review of the Industrial Sociology Unit. Against this background of uncertainty, the chair of Industrial Sociology was advertised and the two of us who emerged as front-runners were existing members of the unit. In the end, no appointment was made, and to avoid — so it was said — making an invidious choice, a senior lecturer was appointed as head of department. This was not a strong position; and in the absence of clear leadership, conflict of both a personal and intellectual kind emerged within the unit. Moreover, the spirit of 1968 was still around with its emphasis on democratic decision making, carried to the point where it was thought possible to develop a research policy by voting. I was not good at handling this situation. Despite the fact that 1969-70 had been spent as a visiting professor at Massachusetts Institute of Technology in the Organizational Behavioral group, the idea that we, in Imperial College, were facing a situation that required "managing" did not occur to me. I made a number of mistakes that troubled me, though fortunately they did not prove fatal to the standing of the discipline or the activity at Imperial.

Indeed the climate was changing outside the college in such a way that the relevance of social science activities to science and technology became more apparent. Increasingly, poor economic performance was linked to the shortcomings of British engineering education and the handicap of the low status associated with the engineering profession. The Industrial Sociology Unit emerged as a key contributor to changes that were considered necessary to improve engineering "formation" at Imperial College. By this time I was the head of the unit, which soon became a full-scale department. My external appointments also continued to multiply rapidly. A key one was being made a member of the council of the main government body controlling the distribution of research funds to the social sciences, where I served for six years. Two other major commitments emerged when I was appointed to membership of a government Royal Commission on the Distribution of Income and Wealth and to the Council of the Arbitration and Conciliation Service, the national body concerned with the resolution of industrial conflict. I think a number of factors contributed to my selection for these appointments. The subject matter of both was central to my own research interests. But the fact that I was a woman also was influential. By this time it was very largely assumed that key public bodies should include at least one woman — the "statutory woman." Whatever the reasons, membership provided a fascinating experience of operating in a political arena.

By the end of the 1970s I felt the need to take stock. It was clear that I was not going to have children. My second marriage had ended. Because of the demands of being head of department, I was spending less and less time on my own research. I therefore jumped at an offer to spend a year on a sabbatical at Oxford University. I had no clear project other than the recharging of my intellectual batteries through access to good libraries and stimulating discussions with distinguished academics in my field. I was aware, however, that I was at a watershed. I was 55; and if I was to change direction, I needed to do so soon. I had already been approached about becoming the head of one or two single-sex women's Oxbridge colleges, but I was not attracted. The canvas appeared too narrow.

There was one other approach that initially I did not consider a starter, but it appeared more interesting as discussions continued. It was to become the head of a rather specialist institution, one of the colleges of London University, spanning the range of university disciplines in its teaching and research. I let my name go forward and to my great surprise was included in a final short list of two. But there I failed, for the selection committee felt that I would not be tough enough (and I think being a woman was a large part of the consideration here) to deal with the major financial problems that were beginning to confront the higher education system. In the light of subsequent developments, there was a certain irony in this. It is possible to argue that in 1981, when I was again approached — this time about becoming the principal of Bedford College, London University — the time was ripe for me to respond positively, which I did in spite of the fact that the Thatcher Government had just announced a major cut in the grant for higher education. But I saw this as a challenge, and so October 1st, 1981, saw me take up the new post.

Bedford College was undoubtedly an institution worth defending. It had been founded in 1849, the first institution to provide university education for women in the country, and had become part of the University of London, created in 1900. Although the teaching staff had always included men, the undergraduate body was single-sex until 1963. Many distinguished academic men and women had brought honor to the college, and its graduates were highly regarded. But it was ill-positioned to face the rigors of the 1980s. It was small (only 1,800 students), it had a large number of departments that in many cases lacked a critical mass, its buildings had not been properly maintained, and the lease on its site in a beautiful location in the middle of Regent's Park in London had only 20 years to run.

As I walked up the stairs to my room on my first day at Bedford, I remember thinking, "You have got to be prepared for a lot of unpopularity; the buck will stop with you in a way it has never done before." How right I was. When I learned the scale of the financial problems that the college faced, I saw that survival as an independent institution was no longer possible. Fortunately, a group of senior academics within the college had already contemplated this possibility, and so we immediately became absorbed in exploring an institutional merger within London University. Speed was of the essence. After a number of false starts, we agreed to merge with Royal Holloway College. It, too, had been a former women-only college. Its academic profile was complementary to that of Bedford, and it was located on a beautiful freehold campus just outside of London with room to expand.

The story of the merger process is a fascinating one. It presented a wide range of management tasks and called for diverse leadership skills. There were complex negotiations with government and the national authorities of higher education to be conducted. There was the need to win the support of London University. There was the academic challenge of developing a vision of what the new combined college could and should be aiming to become in the context of a rapidly changing society. There was the need, initially, to win over vociferous opponents who saw the decision to merge as vandalism; and there was the need to provide a sense of security and purpose to staff and students who experienced traumatic disruption. Communication became a major preoccupation. There was always tension between the need for speedy decisions and the need to provide a mutual understanding of the issues involved.

By the summer of 1985, the legal hurdles had been overcome. Royal Holloway and Bedford New College was born, and I became principal. But difficulties did not disappear overnight. Change was now endemic in the higher education system as a result of government policy, and shortage of resources remained a perennial problem. Up to that point I had had little time to reflect on my management style. I simply drew on my relatively diverse previous experience, which certainly stood me in good stead. But now it seemed to me important to pay more attention to process and to build more formally on the teams that had emerged, whilst at the same time examining my own behavior, which often displayed impatience and, some might say, arrogance. I sought the help of an organizational development consultant, a quite unusual innovation in British universities at that time. She proved immensely helpful. Our first task was to strengthen relationships and to clarify roles within the senior management team. The second was to work with department heads to facilitate the formation and commitment to a medium-term academic strategy for the college. The third was to provide me with a sounding board, if only to make my job less lonely. I wish that I had initiated something along those lines earlier.

I retired in October 1990 at the age of 65. When I am asked whether I miss the job, my answer is "no." It was very stressful, not least because I felt responsibility not only for the survival and success of the institution but also for the individuals, both staff and students, who were involved. But if I am asked whether I enjoyed the nine years in which I did the job, my answer is an emphatic "yes." I experienced the pleasure and exhilaration of working with a group of people who were not only generously supportive but also shared my ideals. The college that has emerged is a success. It now has more than 5,000 students, having been able to grow as a result of changes in government policy towards the expansion of the system. It is not free of financial worries, because that is impossible in the current climate; but it has a wonderful campus and fine new buildings. Most important of all, its reputation for both teaching and research is growing, and the students love it.

Any career has to be understood in context. I lived through a period of immense change, both in the higher education system itself and in attitudes towards women, thanks to the achievements of the women's movement. To say that we still have far to go should not be to deny how far we, as women, have come.

Anne Wright

EMPHASIZE THE POSSIBLE
by Anne Wright

Anne Wright is vice-chancellor of the University of Sunderland. She earned a B.A. Honours and a Ph.D. in English literature from King's College of the University of London. She served as lecturer in English at the University of Lancaster, reader in modern English studies and head of English literature at the Hatfield Polytechnic, and deputy rector at the Liverpool Polytechnic before becoming vice-chancellor and chief executive at the University of Sunderland.

For many years she pursued semi-professional singing in concert and theater performance in parallel to her academic career. Dr. Wright's academic and management distinctions include a British Academy Research Award, the fellowship of the Royal Society of Arts, and the companionship of the Institute of Management. She is a member of the Further Education Funding Council, the Council for Industry and Higher Education, and the National Advisory Council on Education and Training Targets, and a director of the Higher Education Quality Control, the Open Learning Foundation. She chairs the Commission on University Career Opportunity.

I was the youngest of three children, with two brothers considerably older than myself. My father was an engineer who designed paper-making machines. His education had been, like that of many others of his day, by part-time evening study. My mother came from a large family, and her father worked on the Liverpool docks as a wharfinger. Like many of her brothers and sisters, she was extremely intelligent, and she was a gifted writer. She left school at 12 and began work with menial jobs. Her circumstances were such that she could not pursue a place in college. Hence, she gained secretarial qualifications and spent her career as a senior secretary. So it was to be from my generation, on both my mother's and father's sides of the family, that the first university graduates came.

From my earliest years I was considered special, both because I was a long-awaited daughter and the baby of the family and because I was seen to be a gifted child. I read easily by the age of three and always excelled among my peers. I loved reading and puzzling and taught myself the basics of French from a children's encyclopedia. I showed early inclination towards performance arts with a strong and musical voice and a degree of dance and drama talent. I started lessons in drama and elocution at the age of six and continued with this individual tuition for the whole of my school career.

When I was ten and approaching the selective examination that all children then took, I feared failure and spent much time practicing verbal and numerical reasoning. In the event, I gained the top marks in the county. My parents were very proud of their daughter, yet torn between pride in my achievements at school and expectations of what a little girl should be and do. I have photos of me in frilly dresses and white gloves, posing with a splendid dolls' pram. I remember thinking that dolls were very fixed and limited, and I preferred the cuddly animals to whom my imagination could assign personalities and dramatic roles. The most telling photos are the ones where I look disheveled and grubby. I was dimly aware at an early age of differences in expectations. The boys had a Meccano set, but I had to be content with Bayco, a building system for houses, and wooden building blocks. I had gangs of friends who were girls, of course, and I went to girls' schools. For my twelfth birthday I received two presents that clearly were intended as a preparation for the future. My parents gave me a sewing machine, and my mother's lifelong friend, a schoolteacher, gave me a complete edition of Shakespeare. I still have both, but the Shakespeare has been more thoroughly used.

In my first year in sixth form, prolonged absence from school following surgery meant that I missed the entrance examination for Oxford and Cambridge. I did not want to stay an extra year at school, so I applied just to the University of London. My father had conflicting feelings about university education for his daughter and thought he might set me up in a hairdressing business.

I was torn between French and philosophy as a degree course. The main influence on my choice of subject was my robust and ambivalent relationship with the head teacher of my convent school, an Irish scientist nun. We fell out over my choice of degree course, as she favored French, being convinced that philosophy would severely damage my moral, intellectual, and religious development. As a compromise I decided on English, which would, I thought, combine literature and philosophy in a single subject.

Outside the formal school curriculum, my childhood love of ballet had turned to theater and to singing. My voice matured very early, and I began part-time tuition at one of the London conservatories when I was 14. The only real burning ambition I had was to emulate the dramatic intensity of Maria Callas. Perhaps this was because I knew what the star achievement would be in opera, whereas I had no idea of what a comparable achievement might be in a career leading from my academic achievements. I was able to pursue semi-professional singing in concert and theater performance for many years, in parallel to my academic career. When eventually I stopped singing — and stopped very completely — at the age of 35, I felt a great loss. Shortly after that, my ascent up the academic and management career ladder accelerated.

University was a shock to my system, in that for the first time I found an intellectual challenge from my peers; and the scope of the work, too, was a challenge. In the university finals examinations, I gained a First Class honors marks in all ten papers — the top in the university in English, and, so I was told, unprecedented. My tutors appeared surprised at my results — presumably I was a fairly inconspicuous student.

With these results came offers of several postgraduate scholarships: from the university, from King's College; and I also received an unsolicited invitation to study for a Ph.D. in California. I already had decided on a year of teacher training, and my first teaching practice assignment was in a London comprehensive school. The elderly professor who was head of the department summoned me to his office, set out the options, and said I could be a full professor by the age of 40, provided I was not thinking of marrying or having a family. These comments did not at the time seem to strike very deep in me, as I was thinking neither of marriage nor a family nor a professorship. However, over the years, the effect on me of this advice and admonition has deepened and grown, and I have both fulfilled and contradicted the script that was given to me. This professor is one of the mentors whose example or advice has fed into my long-term self-assessment and career planning. The trigger events that I remember have more often been negative experiences that have fired me with resolve to challenge or disprove assumptions.

My final-year specialization had been modern drama, and for my research topic I chose the works of the dramatist George Bernard Shaw, concentrating on his play *Heartbreak House*. I had enjoyed seeing a number of Shaw's plays at the local repertory theater in my teenage years. I also was interested in why the lecturers considered Shaw unworthy of academic research. And I found that literary critics were very divided as to whether *Heartbreak House* was a great achievement or a complete failure. I was fortunate in that I was my supervisor's first doctoral student, and she was both conscientious and kind. Under the terms of one of my scholarships I began teaching as a tutorial assistant. I did not at first think of university teaching as a possible career; but halfway through my second year of full-time research, I decided to apply for a few jobs, one at the very new University of Lancaster. My research supervisor was concerned as to the credentials of this very new "new university," but I decided to take the post.

In retrospect, my career moves always seem to have been a surprise to those around me. When I left Lancaster to move to a very new polytechnic, one of the professors told me to stay no longer than two or three years or it would damage my career. When I eventually left the polytechnic 13 years later to take up a central administrative post after 17 years of teaching and research, and only one year after gaining a readership, some colleagues thought this was a "tragedy." I have found that what seem to me to be opportunities may seem to others to hold no prospects. I did not consciously map out in my career a pathway with several stepping stones towards an identified goal, but at the same time I always have been strongly motivated to strive for the next challenge. For the first 15 years or so, there was never more than a year before I started thinking of applying for promotion or for another post.

I was married after one year at Lancaster. Although my husband was offered teaching posts nearby, we decided it would be more practical to base our two careers in and around London. I applied for all the posts advertised as a lecturer in English, and was offered one at a polytechnic in the south of England near London. The polytechnics had been established in 1969 as an alternative to universities in vocational higher education. Hatfield was starting up its humanities department and just beginning to offer degree courses. My colleagues at Lancaster thought this move was a drop out of an academic career. In this period of growth and development I was able to achieve progressively more senior positions and a range of responsibilities in the polytechnic. I began to be involved in outside committees, especially those of the validating body of the polytechnics, the Council for National Academic Awards.

My daughter was born in 1982, and I returned to work when she was 16 weeks old. I had handed the completed manuscript of a textbook to a publisher as I went into labor. When I returned as a working mother, I found that expectations of me were lower, but this in turn changed my expectations of myself in the opposite direction. Previously I had not been successful in obtaining more senior posts at other polytechnics, so I applied for and was offered a post at the Council for National Academic Awards.

As registrar for Arts and Humanities, I had oversight of the approval and validation of all programs in the polytechnic sector in these fields — about 175 programs and more than 20,000 students. This was a positive career move, because it gave me a national role and overview, and because the post was at a grade equivalent to a senior management post in an institution.

My new post meant a radical change in working style, from academic conditions of service to a largely office-based responsibility but also with frequent travel away from home. We had a succession of nannies until my daughter was older than two, when my husband took our daughter to the creche at his own place of work, the BBC Open University at Milton Keynes. We both believed in shared parenting and in the importance of avoiding stereotyping in bringing up a daughter. As a teacher of science in a girls' school, my husband had developed his views on the position of girls in science, education, and careers. What spurred me on was the increasingly strong feeling that if I was going to be separated from my daughter for large parts of her day in her early life, it really had to be worth it. This motivated me to move swiftly up the hierarchy to senior management.

After a year at CNAA, I applied for two posts as deputy principal at polytechnics and was appointed to the first one that came up, at Liverpool Polytechnic, as deputy rector (academic). This involved moving away from the London area, and so I was separated from my daughter for three months. It meant long weekend journeys — and on one dreadful weekend, no journey at all, which meant a two weeks' separation. This was the final straw, and after that my daughter moved in with me. A nanny was hired, and my husband commuted. Thus one of my few parental achievements is that I was the one who took her on her first day to real school. The other one is that I taught her to read. I remembered my father painstakingly teaching me to read when he came home from work at lunch times, and I was determined that she should read by the time she was three as I had. We played word games and diligently pursued a reading scheme early each morning before I left for work at CNAA and she left for the creche with my husband.

I really enjoyed the senior responsibility, the range and the excitement of my new post at Liverpool, an institution that at the time had 11,000 students. This was the first job in which I had found a complete challenge and satisfaction. There also was a personal feature to working in Liverpool. Although my mother had died in 1980, and she had moved away from Liverpool in the

1920s, I found that in a sense I was coming home. It was perhaps this coming together of past and present that aroused my interest in the history of education for women.

I also became increasingly fascinated by the life of the city and the role that the polytechnic could play in urban regeneration. My arts background gave me the confidence to become involved in theaters and in the arts strategy of the city. I had written down my singing and my experience and interest in drama and the arts on application forms and *curricula vitae* as "other interests," if at all. But suddenly, this long training and range of amateur and semi-professional experience made sense. I could and did apply what was almost in my bones to arts policy, arts management, and arts development across the whole range of the performing arts. I found that I also was comfortable with aspects of organization and people management of the arts, because I was used to a wide range of arts practitioners and arts practice.

I realized, too, that many of the aspects of my post were skills that I could transfer from performance. Many years before I had any formal management training, I had undertaken continuous development in communication, personal effectiveness, people management, and organization skills. This realization has convinced me of the importance of looking at a career portfolio as a whole and considering all life experiences as positive and formative. I have found that many women discount the range of experience that they may have, including substantial experience of home management and family.

Two years or so after I had taken up my post at Liverpool, I was nominated for and accepted into the prestigious Cabinet Office Top Management Programme. This intensive program involves small groups of senior civil servants and senior executives from industry, business, and the professions and is designed for people who have the potential to reach the top of their professions. I was accepted into this program in 1988 and found myself the only woman among 25 participants.

The timing of this strategic management development was especially useful for my then post, as the British polytechnics were soon to become independent corporations with increased financial and management responsibilities. In the program I learned about quality management, the management of change, and other management issues that up to that point I had dealt with without benefit of theory or instruction. The emphasis on strategic planning and the range of personal and organizational success stories that we considered developed my ability to analyze a situation and a problem and decide on a management solution.

The program triggered my desire to move to the top of an organization. During the next 18 months or so I applied for and was short-listed for a small number of posts as principal of a polytechnic. With this final step, I had to learn not only an improved interview technique but also how to approach a top-level appointment, what kind of information to find out, and what the appointing committee needed to know. It is important, particularly in the later stages of an appointment process, to think carefully about the post and to be able to say what you would do in the post if you were appointed — and mean it. Also, because there were few or no role models either for me or for the appointing committees, I had to address the task of being appointed as a woman to the top post.

In March 1989 I was appointed as rector and chief executive of Sunderland Polytechnic in the northeast of England. I was excited by the possibilities that arose from the urban context of industrial change. Sunderland had just lost its shipyards and was facing a new industrial world. However, the region had a history of high unemployment and low participation in further and higher education. I felt as though there was a major role that the polytechnic could play in the community as a resource of expertise and a base for providing the knowledge and skills that would be needed for the future. I had become aware of the way in which organizations can work together for economic, educational, and social development of a community and could see that the ingredients and the players were there in Sunderland and in the region.

My husband and I knew from all our experience of previous career moves that this had to be a complete commitment and a joint decision, which involved a life change for the whole family. My husband was prepared to go freelance as a media producer and to resign his BBC post. My daughter was well-established at her school, and it would be a great wrench for her to leave Liverpool, her home, and friends. We moved in just five months to a new job, a new home, a new life, and a new school for my daughter. Five years on, she is happy, confident, and successful; and my husband has established a small multimedia business of his own. We have become intensely aware, as a family, of our interdependence. I am conscious of what my daughter gets and what she loses by the intensity of my job. I have great respect for the maturity of her approach to having a mother in a senior position. It has drawn us very close together, and I hope that on balance she will in later life still view this as a positive experience.

Since I was appointed chief executive, the polytechnic has grown from 7,000 to over 15,000 students, and since 1992 we have been a university. We have a strong profile in the region, nationally, and internationally. Our support of industry and business in research and applications is extensive and often innovative. We have targeted in our strategic plan the enhancement of quality through development of new methods of teaching and learning, including the potential of the information revolution. Our commitment is to lifelong learning and to the role of the university as a resource and a generator for the development of individuals and the community, working with others to contribute to educational, economic, and cultural development.

Role models are a crucial ingredient in career development. I met Pauline Perry shortly after she had been appointed as director of South Bank Polytechnic, the first woman to hold such a post. I have been encouraged and supported by her example and her friendship since then. We were the only women at the Committee of Directors of Polytechnics. Then, when the polytechnics became universities in 1992, we were the only women with the title vice-chancellor, and joined with Tessa Blackstone at the Committee of Vice-Chancellors and Principals, the CVCP. Assuming the title of vice-chancellor was a significant moment, as the title was overwhelmingly historically male. I can find only one woman who previously held the title, Dame Lilian Penson, who was vice-chancellor of London University in the 1940s.

I have often been asked about what it is like to be the only woman, or one of a very few women, in a senior group. In fact, this has happened to me many times as I have found myself progressing to positions where women have not previously been appointed. Invariably I have found that such pathfinding initially meant dealing with the expectations and assumptions of male colleagues; but equally I have invariably found, after an initial stage of adjustment on their part and a learning curve on mine in the job, that colleagues are supportive and that I can value the support that a network of peers gives. The position in British higher education has nevertheless been that few women have been appointed to senior posts. In 1994, CVCP launched the Commission on Career Opportunity (CUCO), which I chair. The commission aims to support and assist universities in achieving a balanced staff community by appointing, deploying, developing, and promoting people from all sections of the community.

The 14 or so members of the commission are vice-chancellors, chairs of university councils and boards, senior administrators, trade union representatives, and private sector executives and experts with substantial equality experience. The commission was launched in June 1994 with a survey of universities' policies and practices in equal opportunities. We found that universities are committed to developing opportunity, both for business reasons as employers and to reflect their core educational objectives. However, policy runs ahead of practice, and many institutions are less secure in translating policy into effective action. There is no doubt that improvement is needed. A Hansard Report on Women at the Top found that universities in the United Kingdom lag behind other sectors in the proportion of women in senior posts. CUCO has just completed its own survey, which confirms that diversity does not accompany seniority in British universities. But the emphases must be on looking forward and on improvement. From 1990, when I was appointed, to 1994, no woman was appointed to head a university or polytechnic. After Pauline Perry's retirement from South Bank, I was for a long while the only woman vice-chancellor. But in the last 18 months we have seen four women appointed both to "new" universities and, for the first time, to traditional universities — to Keele and East Anglia, two of the "new universities" of the 1960s. At the residential meeting of the vice-chancellors in September 1995, six women out of a hundred or so members were visible, whereas the previous September there were just two.

The ingredients of success in becoming a chief executive or a college president are the same for women as for men. They include determination, the ability to learn from all life experiences, and a sense of humor. I believe that organizations, and ultimately society as a whole, benefit from the increased contribution of women in senior management positions. If there are unnecessary organizational obstacles, such as lack of child care provision, that prevent women from reaching such positions, then we can and should look at how the obstacles can be removed.

Having studied in depth the elaborate persona of "G.B.S." that George Bernard Shaw constructed, I am aware that autobiography is not necessarily synonymous with authenticity. We select the episodes; we construct the story. At the same time, I also have learned the value of women telling their story, both for others and more importantly for themselves. Telling your own success story is part of building your awareness of your achievements and building confidence and direction for the future. And if, like many women, you have no script of success to follow in the sense of no clear pathways or role models, you may have to write the script yourself. The most important hint in writing that script is to learn from the negative and to emphasize the positive.

My own script is indebted to many mentors, both conscious and unwitting, whose positive influence I gratefully acknowledge here.

Judith A. Sturnick

"THE WEB OF OUR LIFE IS OF A MINGLED YARN"

by Judith A. Sturnick

Judith A. Sturnick is the former president of Keene State College (1987-93) and the University of Maine at Farmington (1983-87). She earned a B.A. in English and history (magna cum laude, Phi Beta Kappa) from the University of North Dakota; an M.A. in English from Miami University in Oxford, Ohio; and a Ph.D. in English from Ohio State University. Before her presidencies, she served as a Department Chair and Vice President for Academic Affairs in Ohio and Minnesota, respectively. Her academic honors include honorary degrees from Capital University and Rivier College and a Woodrow Wilson Fellowship.

Dr. Sturnick's numerous articles, books, and invited presentations at professional development programs, such as the Harvard Institute for Educational Management and the Higher Education Resource Services Institutes at Bryn Mawr and Wellesley Colleges, deal with higher education administration, gender and diversity, leadership, and stress management. Since 1993, she has been executive director of a successful consulting firm.

Shakespeare had it right in *All's Well That Ends Well*: "The web of our life is of a mingled yarn, good and ill together." We all take many journeys in our lives. Each of us has an interesting story to tell. Yet, as I sit in my office with the California sun splashed across my computer screen and keyboard, I am puzzled about where to begin in my own narrative. There are so many stories layered within my central story, so many threads tangled around each other, so many versions of the same tale (because perspectives shift and change as years and experience deepen one's understanding), so many events that did not matter nearly so much at the time of the happening as they do in retrospect (and vice versa), and so much of my life still to be lived.

Then, too, there is the matter of how one can encompass the narrative of a complicated life within 4,000 words. Clearly, it must be a subjective and sporadic tale. But there also is the fine art of mystery that veils the storytelling and the teller. How much do I depict? Do I go to my deep heart's core to share what I have come to know about the elements that shaped me? What is really important to define for my audience so that the resonances of my life — like the temple bells hanging above my bed — ring true? What odyssey brought me from the North Dakota tundra and the glorious lakes of Minnesota to Ohio, South Carolina, Maine, New Hampshire, Massachusetts, and — finally — to California, which I love as only a geographically born-again convert can? Like many good stories, mine begins *in medias res*. When I was 12 years old, I remember sitting on the black boulder that was my favorite spot in the woods, overlooking the Minnesota River, composing a poem and feeling electric with a sense of destiny. The clarity was absolute: My life had a mission toward which many strong forces would propel me — to teach, to write, and to lead. From that point on, I knew that my piece of the universal equation was to obtain as much education as I could, to have a heart and mind eager to learn, and to present myself fully to life. Through many difficult times of pain, abuse, and grief — which are not necessary to detail for this telling — I was sustained by that inner knowing. I trusted the universe then, and I trust it now.

To that young girl, an extraordinary life has been given, with truly incredible happenings. Not only did I serve for nearly 11 years as the president of two campuses (and for quite a long period of time I was one of only five women who had gone on to a second presidency), but I have traveled the world from Lithuania to Egypt, read scholarly papers at international meetings, chaired and served on national boards and commissions, published books and articles, delivered hundreds of speeches for audiences of thousands, was selected the outstanding professor at my campus, been awarded two honorary doctorates, met the most prominent people from all walks of life (poets, politicians, U.S. presidents, movie stars, authors, corporate CEOs, journalists), and received more awards and plaques than I can recall.

For all that, it has not been the titles and honors that matter. Instead, my life's meaning boils down to having the power to make a positive difference in the lives of others. Authentic power springs from the opportunities to mentor others, to set aside budget dollars to send them to the Bryn Mawr Institute and the Harvard Institute for Educational Management, to find ways to promote individuals internally on the campus, to inspire students (especially women) to dream more dramatic dreams, to help create a collegiate community, to rebuild a campus burdened by decades of deferred maintenance, to leave human and intellectual legacies, and to have loved — and been loved — by many people in the process.

Education made all this possible. My paternal grandfather emigrated from Sweden, and my grandmother was born here into a Swedish family that had recently immigrated. Although not formally educated, they — like many other Scandinavian newcomers in the Upper Midwest — believed in the efficacy of education. When my grandmother had to quit school in the sixth grade in order to help full-time on the farm, she said her heartfelt goodbye to the one-room schoolhouse by lovingly scrubbing the floor on her hands and knees one Sunday afternoon. Despite this, she gave me the gift of her love of poetry, which she could recite from memory by the hour; and my grandfather, who had only a fourth grade education, sang in his warm tenor voice and gave me a love of music and opera.

Those Swedish grandparents were my first important role models, ambitious for me to have the education that they could not attain and convinced that I would achieve many things. It helped that I was born on Easter Sunday, a sign for grandma that I was a special child with a sunlit future. I often have wondered whether I was just lucky enough to have been born to lead or whether her strong conviction created that reality in my own mind. Whatever the case, the result was the same. And years later, when I was ten years old and my father was attending college on the G.I. Bill, he would open his textbooks at random, point to a page, and say, "Read this out loud." After I had finished, he would ask, "Now, tell me what you just read." Thus I learned vocabulary and developed comprehension far beyond my years and gained the ability to articulate what I knew. I also gained the love of books. Destiny? Yes, by dint of circumstance, nurturing, and native common sense.

The Scandinavian influence on my life was — and still is — important. My California home is filled with Swedish mementos, many of them from my grandparents. One of my keenest memories is playing Swedish music on the piano (my grandparents started my lessons when I was in the first grade) as grandpa sang the melodies of the Old Country (such as "Varmeland" and "Var Vindar Kriska" — songs I still play today on my cherished baby grand), with tears of longing and nostalgia running down his cheeks. As much as they revered America, they taught me that my genetic heritage was one of strength, resoluteness, duty (ah, that Lutheran background!), self-discipline, and "calling" (a concept I still live by today). In instilling those principles, they also gave the context of the wider world as a frame of reference.

I have been talking about education in general. Now let me be more specific about my own. All my degrees are in English, that most versatile and inclusive field. Not only was it a rich subject to teach at the college level, but it taught me about human nature, psychology, philosophy, faith, integration, and synthesis. It was the perfect discipline to prepare me for the rest of my life, from teaching to administration to running a resort to working with battered wives and displaced homemakers to my current work as a consultant and professional coach for executives.

Although I taught at both private and public institutions, my own degrees are all from public universities: the University of North Dakota, Miami University (Ohio), and Ohio State University. Because it always seemed to me that time was of the essence, I went straight through all my degrees without stopping out, and all of my learning was financed by scholarships and fellowships (a Woodrow Wilson Fellowship and a three-year National Defense Fellowship at the graduate level).

I firmly believe that the education that transformed my life has the same power for every individual. Had public universities not been accessible and affordable, had generous scholarship help not existed, my path would have been much more difficult. Consequently, just as my grandmother scrubbed the schoolroom floor to give gratitude back for her education, I have in different ways gratefully attempted to live my life so that I could open doors and provide both opportunities and encouragement for others. To give back what one has been given was one of grandma's dictates that I still try to honor daily.

Of course, mentors throughout my life have been generous, perceptive, and loving in their guidance. I especially remember the high school English teacher who was enthusiastic over a short story I had written, my debate coach who taught me to think and speak on my feet (great skills for any university president), the gentle man who prompted me through my master's thesis at a time when I feared that my University of North Dakota degree had not prepared me well enough to do graduate work at sophisticated Miami University, the senior faculty member who took me under her wing during my first job, the chancellor who held me up to standards high enough to turn me from a good president into a first-rate one, and too many others to mention. Even now, I have mentors. As I have launched a new career in consulting, two colleagues are teaching me the best of what they know about being effective and successful in the new arena.

It may well be true that one never outgrows a need for mentors. There are always so many new skills, new learning, new comprehensions about the world and people to take in; and the guidance of individuals who have already walked the path and gained the insights is of immeasurable help. So, too, it is true that one never outlives the ability to offer useful mentoring to others. We *do* learn by teaching, and mentoring is rarefied teaching. When I draw my last breath, I hope it will be for two purposes: to give thanks for this quite special life I have led and to offer a last insight to a mentee. Well, perhaps I am being a bit supercilious about the last part of that sentence, but it makes a point.

During these years of leadership, I also have learned that mentoring is especially important for women to offer to other women. We need male mentors, too; but women understand the language and realities of other women in a unique way. It may even be that female mentors help us work our way through the long struggles we have with our mothers. Whatever the case, those of us who have been fortunate enough to open and walk through doors formerly closed have a sacred obligation to hold that door open for the women who follow us. If the gains we have made personally and professionally are to have any deeper meaning, it is to hold the place we have reached until other women can go beyond our accomplishments to set a new pace for the future.

Years ago I read a book about the importance of mentoring for young men. I still vividly recall the author's statement that the purpose of mentoring is to assist a man "to realize his dream." That is a phrase both beautiful and powerful. This is what we as women leaders need to do for each other, assisting not only in the realization of the dream but also creating the environment in which women can dare to dream in the first place.

Thus far, I have talked about the things that shaped my life and work: my family and Swedish background, education, music, writing, generous mentoring, a still insatiable desire to learn and to teach, the self-discipline to shape my innate gifts, and a sense of "calling." Certainly I have had bountiful luck and grace in my life. Luck and grace, however, must be complemented by ethical integrity and courage in effective leadership. There is, naturally, a story within a story here, too. Several years ago, when I was the president of a public campus in New Hampshire, I walked out of my staff meeting one morning to find my public relations director in a dither. "Have you heard the news?" she asked breathlessly. "No," I replied, puzzled. "Well, the governor just demanded your resignation."

Needless to say, there was the beat of a very long pause. "Huh?" I said cogently. It was a totally dumbfounding moment. "What for?"

"He says," she explained, "that you are a godless leader and that Keene State is a godless campus because you have moved the baccalaureate ceremony off campus."

Even as I now write about this event, I am still dumbfounded. After three years of discussion at the college, we agreed that the heavily religious ceremony should be retained but moved to a nearby church in order, appropriately, to maintain the separation of church and state. At that point — when the former governor, John Sununu, was the chief of staff in the Bush White House — the President was about to give a major speech at Ann Arbor, Michigan, against church/state separation. New Hampshire may have seemed like fertile ground for an opening salvo in the debate. (The Supreme Court was also soon to hear a test case on the issue.)

It was clear that this was not a local matter but one that was firmly connected to national politics and pre-presidential campaign publicity. Of course, I ignored the demand for my resignation and worked with the board of trustees to strategize ways of saving face for the governor and cooling down the issue. However, the governor had his own momentum under way, and the next day he held another press conference insisting that the trustees fire me. Behind-the-scenes negotiations were ineffective, and by now both the governor and I were besieged by reporters from CNN, CBS and NBC, Public Broadcasting, and major newspapers across the country. In my home states of North Dakota and Minnesota, I made daily headlines. It was indeed an affair to remember.

There was quite a bit of pressure on me to back down, apologize to the governor, and return baccalaureate to campus. Additionally, there was strong political pressure not to defy the governor and to bow out gracefully. Standing in that searchlight of national publicity and living in a state very much controlled politically by the party of the governor, if ever there was a time in my life when I had to trust myself and my integrity, this was it.

Following my own well-attended press conference, in which I made it clear that I would not resign and that these were principles too significant to forsake, the tide of public opinion turned in my favor. Letters, even in the governor's office, ran three to one against him. By the end of a tense week, not unlike the showdown at the OK Corral, he backed down. Two years later, at a large public banquet, he delivered an elegant apology. That was an unexpected bonus.

The bottom line here is this: There are times in one's life when a person has to be willing to put his or her job on the line in order to preserve one's principles. That is not a cliché, and it happens to leaders more often than one might think. Whatever the outcome may be, there is dignity in knowing that one has the tools to handle anything, that fear need not overwhelm, and that integrity is not for barter under any circumstances.

The story of my confrontation with the governor leads logically into portraying some of the tougher realities of my life and leadership. In what I have said so far, it may seem as if everything came easily to me. That is never the case for anyone, though it may look like that from the outside. Our strength, toughness, and resilience come from being willing to undertake the journey through rocky hills, sere wastelands, and buffeting winds. We all take that journey periodically, and I have come to value these times for the testing of my mettle and the leaps in courage that result. The question always is, during even the harshest times, "What is the learning here?" My questing life is a spiritual odyssey, and the discovery of my own soul is what I pursue.

Does that sound a bit odd coming from someone who now works as a consultant-coach? Not really. In a congruent life every part fits into the whole. The ethical principles that governed me through the crazy times of my life are my foundation now. The authenticity that has come sometimes so painfully and slowly, through times of intense confusion, also makes my work authentic. I teach, I lead, I write, as I have always done. And always with the question — both haunting and comforting — "What is the learning here?"

The sinew behind that query comes from the experiences I wish to share now, one of which is my own lifelong battle with addiction. Part of the pain and grief of my early life was the result of generations of addiction (there surely is a genetic component to this disease) on both sides of my family. For a period of 12 of my adult years, I was a full-blown, secret drinker who was sick with shame over the hold alcohol had on my life. It controlled what I did, how I felt about myself (awful!), how I spent my money, and how I viewed the world.

It is not necessary to tell the story with gruesome details, though there are plenty of those. It is enough to say that I finally had to make a choice, literally, between life and death. Had I gone on drinking, I would not be here today. Someone who has not experienced the hold a substance can have over a person's life may not understand what it means to give it up. Bluntly put, it was terrifying. However, with a great deal of help and frequent 12-step meetings, I have now been "clean and sober," as the posters say, for 14 years. And I have been graced with the opportunity to help others get, and stay, sober over those years.

This part of my story is important for many reasons. The academic culture is plagued by alcohol abuse that we deny and cover up, much to the detriment of campus community and the learning environment. Many of my colleagues at all levels, including presidents, wage sad and lonely fights with this disease; and countless lives are devastated by its impact. My story also has meaning because it took courage and toughness to deal with my addiction.

Several years after I put aside the alcohol, I discovered that I had replaced it, as not infrequently happens, with an addiction to work. As time passed, I began to overwork on a grand scale.

What was the learning here? The learning was, I need to say, totally gut-wrenching. I had to confront the mental processes and character flaws that could so easily substitute one substance (work) for another (alcohol) and keep the internal addictive systems in place. Not unexpectedly, once I allowed myself to slow down the work frenzy, I crashed. I was burnt up and flamed out.

My learning this time was how to deal with all of it — the burnout, the question of what was I doing with my life, the anguish of wondering what was my right livelihood, the fear and humiliation

I felt when I resigned from my presidency in order to heal. Just as recovering from physical burns is an agonizing time, so is recovering from emotional and spiritual burnout. However, there also have been wonders and joys in the recovery from burnout. My spiritual life has once again come alive with renewed sense of a "call" to work. I have learned again to meditate, to take care of myself, to say no, to trust myself, to live by faith, to have a passion for my work *and* my life, to hold my energy, and to serve the spirit of the universe. Part of my work now is leading workshops on stress, and much of my professional coaching focuses on helping leaders avoid burning out. In this way, I am turning.

One of the most meaningful lessons has been about forgiveness. We can forgive the actions of people who have brought pain into our lives, forgive the past, forgive ourselves. There is immense strength in the act of forgiveness — as well as liberation. This came home to me anew two years ago when, after a considerable time of estrangement, my father and I reconnected. Following a cycle of amends and forgiveness, we have been able to move on together, and I have found a filial love for which I had given up hope. In an even richer blessing, I not only regained my father, but a nurturing new mother as well.

It is true that we are as much shaped by the hands of adversity as we are by the hands of grace. Therefore, one of the greatest gifts we can give each other as women leaders and potential leaders is to tell each other the truth of our individual lives, instead of our gilded, self-serving myths. We get where we are by having the courage to walk both the dark paths and the light paths. My life has been wonderful, as well as marked with grief.

Leadership is an act of continuous creation. Because what works in one circumstance may not be effective in another, the lessons of today may be partially obsolete tomorrow. New paradigms confront us every moment and demand our best impulses. The most effective role models reveal their true selves so that we may emulate the best and learn compassion from the flaws.

We do indeed take many journeys in our lives. It is the spirit in which we journey that, in the end, makes all the difference.

About the Author

Karen Doyle Walton is vice president for academic affairs and professor of mathematics at Allentown College of St. Francis de Sales. She earned degrees in mathematics from Vassar College, Harvard University, and the University of Pittsburgh, and a doctorate in higher education administration from Lehigh University. She previously chaired the mathematics departments of two colleges before assuming her current position.

Dr. Walton's inservice courses for teachers of mathematics, science, and computer science have received more than $1 million in funding from the U.S. Department of Education, the Pennsylvania Department of Education, and other sources. She has published more than 30 articles in a variety of journals. The focus of her writing has been on computer applications to the teaching of mathematics and encouraging girls and minority students in mathematics, science, and technology.

DATE DUE